HIRING
3.0

New Rules For The New Economy

BARRY SHAMIS

ISBN: 0615421644
ISBN-13: 9780615421643
LCCN: 2010941381

About The Author

Barry Shamis is the CEO of Selecting Winners, an international management consulting company that solves strategic staffing issues. He founded Selecting Winners in 1984. He has worked with more than 400 companies from almost every industry. Some of his clients include Cisco Systems, SAP, Oracle, The St. Paul Companies, AT&T, Texas Instruments, and many more.

Barry Shamis has delivered more than 1900 presentations in 50+ countries on the subjects of recruiting, selection and retention. He has received the highest earned designation "the Certified Speaking Professional" as awarded by the National Speakers Association. He was recently voted into the hall of fame by an organization of more than 9000 CEO's.

Barry Shamis has written hundreds of articles that have appeared in journals and top online publications. He has been featured on ABC News 20/20 and in the Wall Street Journal. He has been a guest lecturer at the University of California at Berkeley and St Marys College.

Barry Shamis is simply one of the most sought-after speakers on the subjects of recruiting, selection and retention.

In the event you would like to reach Barry Shamis the best way is through email at BarryShamis@gmail.com

Table of Contents

Foreword 1

Chapter 1 New Staffing Challenges..................................3

Chapter 2 History of Hiring 7

Chapter 3 Common Hiring Problems 9

Chapter 4 Why Hire? 15

Chapter 5 Recruiting..17

    Part 1 Recruiting Philosophy 17

    Part 2 Recruitment Planning......................................22

    Part 3 Sourcing..25

    Part 4 Social Media..31

Chapter 6 Screening 33

    Part 1 Screening Overview...33

    Part 2 Reading Resumes...37

    Part 3 Phone Screen...43

    Part 4 Video Screening 45

Chapter 7 Testing & Assessment.....................................47

Chapter 8 Achievement-based Profile 51

Chapter 9 The Behavioral Model 59

Chapter 10 Interview Questions 63

    Part 1 Characteristics of Effective Questions 63

Part 2 Types of Effective Questions.............................67

Part 3 Creating Questions 71

Part 4 EARs 75

Part 5 The Interview Guide 79

Part 6 Questions to Avoid 83

Chapter 11 The Face-to-Face Interview...................87

Part 1 The Interview Setting 87

Part 2 The Opening..89

Part 3 Controlling the Interview.............................93

Part 4 Interviewing Tips...95

Part 5 Problem Situations.......................................99

Part 6 Closing the Interview.................................103

Chapter 12 Marketing the Position.........................107

Chapter 13 Checking References 109

Chapter 14 Background Checks..............................113

Chapter 15 The Hiring Decision 115

Chapter 16 Making the Offer 119

Chapter 17 Getting the Person On Board 121

Appendix A Sample Interview Questions.................123

Appendix B Achievement-based Profile Form..........125

Disclaimer

The information is this book is offered with the understanding that it does not contain legal, financial, or other professional advice. Individuals requiring such services should consult a competent professional.

The author and publisher make no representation about the suitability of the information contained in this book for any purpose. This material is provided "as-is" without warranty of any kind.

Although every effort has been made to ensure the accuracy of the contents of this book, errors and omissions can occur. The publisher assumes no responsibility for any damages arising from the use of this book, or alleged to have resulted in connection with this book.

This book is not completely comprehensive. Some readers may wish to consult additional books for advice.

Foreword

Why write a book on hiring employees? The reason I wrote this book is because the most important decision any business owner or manager ever makes is deciding who is going to work for them.

I've been teaching companies how to hire for more than 35 years. In every organization I have ever spoken to, the first question asked is, "Who's had any formal training on how to hire people?" The percentage of answers has stayed reasonably consistent for more than 35 years. About 10% of the room raises their hand and acknowledge they have taken a course or seminar, or they've read a book on how to hire new employees.

When you stop and think about all the assets in your business, it is generally agreed the most important asset is your people. If the most important asset is your people, and yet less than 10% of people have ever been trained on how to make a hiring decision, it is easy to see why consistently hiring successful employees remains a problem.

The other reason I decided to write this book is the promise of a better life. Doesn't that sound pie in the sky? It is an undeniable truth that life gets a whole lot better when you have great employees. Talk to any of my clients, especially those who "have gotten religion" about hiring great employees, and the consistent message heard is they enjoy their business more.

Almost all of the typical problems disappear when a business has the right person in the right job at the right time doing the right things. Coming to work in the morning becomes a joy. Why? Because by eliminating people problems you get to work on the kinds of problems that are fun: acquiring customers, developing products and solutions and services—those are the fun problems. Dealing with people problems is no one's idea of fun.

Have you ever heard anyone say, "I cannot wait to get out of bed in the morning, get into the office, and manage a hiring mistake?" You probably won't hear that statement anytime soon.

The promise of a better life simply means your whole business life gets easier when great employees are hired.

At the beginning of all of my workshops, the Managers and Business Owners have always heard the same claim:

1. Get good at hiring people, and life gets easy. There are a lot less problems. A majority of business problems disappear when you've got good employees. And, the problems you do work on are more enjoyable and more profitable.

2. The second reason it pays to get good at hiring is to make more money. The best businesses usually have the best employees. If it is your business, you are going to make more money. Profits are going to be greater. If you are working for an organization as a manager, your department will be more successful. As a result you will get recognized for that success, you will get raises, and you will get promotions. It is that simple.

The reason to get good at recruiting and selecting employees is for a better life and to make more money.

Chapter One

New Staffing Challenges

The business world has changed. There are new problems, new circumstances and new challenges. The historical solutions no longer apply. The number one challenge brought on by these changes is *unpredictability*. Unpredictability drives most managers and business owners absolutely crazy.

There are a number of factors contributing to the rise of unpredictability. First and foremost, is the pace of change. The pace of change business owners and managers face today is much greater than it has been historically. We used to write five and ten year strategic plans. Now we write five- and ten-month strategic plans because the pace of change has increased so dramatically.

Most business models work because the market conditions and competitors are well understood. By understanding assets, strengths and weaknesses, plans can be developed that offer the best opportunity to succeed.

However in today's marketplace, competition has taken on a new face. There are more and nontraditional competitors. Historically, competitors were easy to identify. There were half a dozen or so companies in your industry that were primary competitors. It was fairly straightforward to follow them, plan and adjust as necessary.

Today, competition is global. New competitors that were never on the radar are very real. Competitors are appearing from other industries as well. Technology has enabled competitors by lowering the barrier to entry in many industries. These non-traditional competitors are a major factor contributing to unpredictability.

Another problem is the entire planning process has not adapted to the pace of change and unpredictability. The best example of this concept is the implementation of forward-looking versus historical issues.

Most business planning makes use of trailing indicators. The primary considerations have been historical results. The most important data points have included: last month's results, what was accomplished the year before and so on. The two most obvious data points are sales and expenses.

All of this information comes from trailing indicators. It was achieved based on historical conditions.

Trailing indicators are less effective when conditions are changing so quickly. The strategies and tactics that worked so well previously may not be as effective given the new set of challenges.

The result is that past business models may not work today or tomorrow.

Leading Indicators

Here are just a few of the considerations that need to be factored into your planning in the new economy:

Pipeline Quality

Your sales forecasts now become more critical given the changing environment. Analyze the make-up and quality of your sales projections. Specifically, look how each opportunity is aligned with your product or solution. Look for compelling events as an indicator of the quality of the forecasted business. And consider the key differentiators your organization brings to the opportunity.

The quality of the sales forecast is a leading indicator. The more reliable the numbers, the better the business plan.

Customer Indicators

The stability and make-up of a client base is critical to future planning. What percentage of clients are repeat buyers? The higher the number of repeat clients, the more reliable the projections. This is a solid leading indicator of the health of a business.

In addition to repeat customers, how loyal are your customers? Satisfied customers become repeat customers. Repeat customers are the most loyal customers. The greater percentage of customers that are loyal, the more insulated the business against new competitors.

These are just a couple of leading indicators that need to be a more integral part of the planning process if you are going to compete in the new economy.

How does this apply to hiring?

It is not possible to succeed in the new economy without a winning business model. A key component of a winning business model is the plan for human assets. A good human asset plan includes not just how many people to hire, but also the types of knowledge, skills and behaviors the new employees need to deliver business objectives.

And, the talent needs to be found, attracted and hired as fast as possible with the least amount of resources spent. The old wives tale, "Hire Slow and Fire Fast" will definitely doom a business in the new economy. Satisfying business needs slowly is a losing strategy.

Here are a couple of specific examples of issues that must be addressed in the new economy to succeed at hiring.

First and foremost, applicant pools are completely different. Massive applicant pools are now normal. Unemployment is at higher levels and will probably stay above historical levels. As a result, more people are applying for jobs. These new applicants are coming from industries that have gone out of business or don't exist anymore. In addition, the fact that more people are transferring industries further complicates matters.

The traditional model of "candidate" no longer exists. Finding the right person is more difficult because there are more people available, and they may not be from the traditional direct competitor.

Also, the pace of change forces a new and critical look at the employment relationship. In the ideal world it would be great to hire a person, have them stay for 30 years, and finally give them a gold watch. That world doesn't exist anymore.

The employees who help solve today's problem may not be the right assets to solve tomorrow's problem. As a result, employment relationships need to evolve.

This real-world problem requires a new paradigm about hiring employees. It is time to treat the employee relationship in a completely new way.

The only reason to enter into an employee relationship is so the employee can satisfy a business need. View this relationship the same as any other business contract. The business needs a result. The employee wants a salary, benefits and an environment where they can succeed.

Both parties have a responsibility to make the contract successful. As long as the person continues to provide positive value to the company they continue to receive money and benefits. This simple model keeps everything in perspective. The contract ends if either side no longer performs their responsibilities.

In the new economy, the employment relationship needs to be mutually beneficial. The focus of the relationship needs to be clearly defined and in place only as long as both sides benefit.

The new economy calls for new and different planning and a new employment relationship.

Chapter Two

History of Hiring

It is critical to understand the history of hiring. The traditional solution has been to throw people at problems. If there is a problem in a business, the solution has been to hire new people. If those people don't work, hire more people and throw them at the problem. This cycle repeats continuously.

It is no wonder there have been large swings in employment over the years. During good times, businesses hired too many employees. When times got tough, the pattern was to get rid of a whole bunch of people, usually too many. The result has been wild fluctuations in the number of employees.

Throwing people at problems hasn't worked in the past and it certainly will not work in the new economy.

Another technique that has plagued hiring through history is trial and error. Think about when you first became a manager. Most likely, early in the new job you had to hire a new employee. What did you do? Most people do the same thing that was done to them. You ask the same questions that were asked. Sometimes you try new techniques; some worked, some didn't. This trial and error tends to go on for a long time. You might still be in the middle of the trial and error stage.

Think about the number of mistakes that have haunted your business as a result of trial and error. The new economy doesn't allow for this unproductive path. The carrying costs are way too high.

Let's look at the hiring problems for a typical sales organization. The first problem is the hiring philosophy. Too often, the organization will hire three or four new employees and hope one works out. I once had a Vice President of an insurance agency brag to me how in their last recruiting class they had a "stick rate" of 35%. He was actually proud of making 65% mistakes.

The next hiring problem is the typical sales organization is a victim of Pareto's Rule. This is the 80/20 principle where 80% of production is from 20% of the salespeople. That means 80% of your salespeople are not carrying their weight. Once again, given the rules of the new economy, the carrying costs are too high.

In the old economy these mistakes were masked by volume. It is easier to hide hiring mistakes when hiring lots of new employees. However, in today's reality, the typical business is not going to hire ten new employees. They will hire one or maybe two new employees.

It is almost impossible to hide a mistake behind volume because the days of volume hiring are gone. The trial and error model can't be used anymore. And, it is no longer acceptable to throw people at problems.

Hiring needs to be as close to perfect as possible in the new economy.

Chapter Three

Common Problems

There are a lot of problems associated with hiring. The problems fall into two categories. First are random errors. These are errors made at random points throughout the process. They are very difficult to identify and correct.

The focus in this book is on the second category of hiring problems. These are systemic problems. Systemic problems arise when the process is flawed. They are repeated continuously in every hiring situation.

Here are some of the more common systemic problems associated with hiring.

Business Issue is Not Defined

The only reason to hire an employee is to satisfy a business need. This will be discussed in great detail later in the book. The truth is people often hire as a knee-jerk reaction. When a key person resigns, the first reaction is to hire a new person. A new employee is hired when you are working too hard. A new employee is hired when a headcount is budgeted. These may or may not be the right moves.

The reason to hire is to satisfy a business need. Whenever the subject or thought of hiring emerges, the first step is to determine the business need that needs to be satisfied. Frame the issue and look at a variety of options to deliver the sought after result. Determine how to best manage a solution. The best solution may be to solve the problem with technology. Or, outsourcing might be the right solution. Eliminating the position might be an option. And sometimes the best decision is to hire a new employee.

Only think about hiring a new employee after clearly defining the business need and determining a new employee is the best solution for the specific business need.

The chances of hiring the right person are pretty slim without the business issue being clearly defined. It is very difficult to know the right person was hired without a clear vision of the business need the person will address. Failing to define your business issue can often doom your process from the start.

Think of this problem as being just slightly off course at the beginning of a journey. The farther you travel, the farther off course you get until you are completely lost.

Making Decisions Out of Frustration

Everyone has been frustrated with the hiring process at one time or another. In addition, most people have been frustrated with a business need not being addressed. These frustrations lead to "settling" for the next candidate to walk through the door.

Frustration can lead to intense pain. Working long hours and harder than normal is not fun. It hurts when things are not getting done in the business. And losing money or customers never feels good. These are just some of the conditions that initiate the hiring process.

Here is a story that illustrates how I was a victim of frustration.

I had just been hired into my first management job. I was put in charge of a recruiting organization, and needed to hire an administrator for the department. I followed the script perfectly. The ad I ran was very good. The response was excellent with lots of candidates. The applicants were screened and narrowed to a manageable number. The interviews were scheduled for the following week. After a solid week of interviewing, the right person had not yet surfaced. It was now frustration/desperation time.

The very last interview was scheduled for Friday afternoon. The thought of starting over was something I could not face. I was really beat up because of the long hours on the new job and was starting to wilt under the weight of the decision.

The last candidate to enter my office was a very nice young lady. She walked into the office and before I could even ask a question, she said, *"I want this job, and you are going to give me this job."* My kind of person! I didn't do much interviewing after that because I could feel my pain going away. Boy, did I live to regret that decision! I hired out of frustration, and made a huge hiring mistake.

Unfortunately, hiring out of frustration is always a problem. The only reason to hire is you are absolutely convinced the person will satisfy the business need.

Making Decisions by Gut-feel

Without a clear process to gather and evaluate the data to make quality, hiring decisions, you are left relying on gut-feel. We all trust our gut. It is hard to argue against. But there is very little science behind gut-feel.

The primary reason people use gut-feel to make hiring decisions is lack of training. Remember, only 10% of people have been taught how to hire new employees. Gut-feel is the default decision-making mechanism without the benefit of proven process.

Here is how gut-feel effects hiring decisions in the real world. A person walks in your office and enthusiastically pumps your hand, and looks you right in the eye. Based on a wonderful first impression and of course a good feeling, the "halo effect" takes over and the person ends up being hired.

The decision was made by gut-feel. It wasn't made on facts. It wasn't made on data. It wasn't been made as a result of a rigorous data-gathering, data-evaluation methodology. It was just a gut-feel saying, "This is a good person."

Sometimes the gut-feel is right. Some people have great instincts. But even if your instincts are outstanding, a rigorous process makes the decisions that much better. In the new economy any hiring mistake might be fatal.

Decisions Are Made Too Quick or Too Slow

Some hiring decisions are made too quickly and some too slowly. Let's talk about the hiring decision made too quickly first. A study was done looking at how quickly people make up their mind in an interview. The results showed better than 60% of all people made up their mind in two minutes or less. In addition, more than 80% of all hiring decisions are made inside of five minutes. This is scary.

How is it possible to get enough data in two or five minutes to make a quality hiring decision? It isn't. From the previous discussion we know most hiring decisions are based on gut-feel and first impressions. The bottom line is most hiring decisions are made for all the wrong reasons.

Hiring decisions need to be made on large quantities of data. Asking lots of effective questions and using a proven data gathering process is critical to effective decisions.

On the other side of the discussion is the problem of hiring decisions being made too slowly. This "analysis to paralysis" is counterproductive. To best serve the business, new employees need to be hired as fast as possible. This may sound strange and seem like the importance of due diligence is being diminished. Not true. A rigorous, methodical due diligence is always necessary but hiring decisions need to be made as fast as possible.

This goes to the heart of hiring to satisfy a business need. Business needs have to be addressed as quickly as possible. Everyday the problem persists, the business is losing money or opportunity. The new economy only exacerbates the problem.

People are taking longer to make hiring decisions because there are more candidates. But regardless of economic conditions, once the decision to add a new employee is made it has to be completed as quickly as possible. The key is to execute the hiring process as quickly as possible without violating the process.

Asking The Wrong Interview Questions

Why do people ask the wrong questions in an interview? The reason is most people don't know which questions are right. There is a lot of misinformation about interview questions causing confusion. Later in the book there is a large chapter covering effective types of questions that should be asked in the interview.

Control of the interview is lost when the wrong questions are asked. Bad questions result in responses full of opinions instead of facts. Bad interview questions don't result in data to help predict success on the job. Bad interview questions lead to all kinds of problems. Consistently asking the wrong questions leads to consistently getting the wrong information.

And consistently getting the wrong information consistently leads to making bad hiring decisions.

The No B.S. Detector

Candidates are taught to tell you exactly what they think you want to hear (the canned answer). Most books for people looking for jobs promote this strategy. From a candidate's perspective, it is a pretty good strategy. Delivering the answer they think you want usually works.

Unfortunately, the canned answer seldom contains the data needed to make a quality hiring decision. The reason this candidate strategy works is because the interviewer is asking the wrong types of questions.

A good B.S. detector has to distinguish between three categories of misinformation. The first category is the candidate sharing what they think you want to hear. Second category is the candidate flat-out fabricating an answer. Sometimes people just fabricate experience or results. That is a huge problem and derails the process.

The last category is when the person is just stretching the truth. A great example of a stretch is when the person uses the word *"we"*. People can be inclusive using the word *"we"* and cover an awful lot of ground. The statement, *"We* put the first man on the moon" is a good example. Who was it specifically that did put a man on the moon? It was NASA, but it was also the United States of America, and the person is an American. Technically the statement is not a lie. However the use of the word *we* certainly did mislead. It is not exactly a fabrication, but it certainly stretches the truth.

Having a B.S. detector solves these problems. Without it you don't get good data and make more mistakes than necessary. The good news is a proven selection process is the best B.S. detector.

These are just a handful of the common systemic errors made in the hiring process. Unfortunately, a flawed process leads to the same mistakes being repeated.

Chapter Four

Why Hire?

"Why hire employees at all?" may seem like a strange question in a book about hiring employees, but the truth of the matter is most people hire for the wrong reasons.

Mary is one of the top performers in the company. She walks into the office and resigns. For whatever reason, Mary is now gone. The typical, knee-jerk reaction is to replace Mary and fill the open position. Unfortunately, most people hire to fill positions. On the surface, this seems to make sense. However a closer examination shows it makes no sense at all.

Let's revisit this situation. Mary has resigned. Instead of the knee-jerk reaction to replace Mary, the better solution is to take the time to evaluate the situation and identify the real business need. It may be determined replacing Mary is not the right decision. The best solution might be to leave the position vacant. It might be to upgrade the position. The decision could be to downgrade the position or even split the position into two positions.

There are many possibilities. The correct option is always the one that satisfies the business need. **The only reason you ever hire someone is to satisfy a business need**. Let's look at this closely because hiring to satisfy business needs is at the heart of strategic staffing in the new economy.

A business develops needs as it grows, as market conditions change and the business model changes. These business needs must be satisfied if the business is going to prosper. There are always multiple ways to satisfy a business need. Using the old model, the default choice was to throw people at the problem. In the new economy a more strategic approach is required.

Once the business need is identified and clearly framed, the decision might be to solve it with technology. A piece of software might deliver the same or better results than a new employee. The most economically solution might be to outsource the work. It may be a short-term issue where hiring a consultant or a contractor is the best way to satisfy the need.

Hiring a full-time employee should not be the first option. Look at every other option first. This strategy works best if satisfying business needs is the focus as opposed to just hiring people. The distinction may seem minor but is really significant.

An effective way to focus thinking on hiring to satisfy business needs is to view people as human assets. Think about solving business problems and issues with assets. Sometimes the assets are technology. A computer or a machine or a piece of equipment is the asset that best satisfies the particular business need. Sometimes a human asset is the best solution to address the particular problem.

Once the decision is made to use a human asset to address the business need, don't just run out and hire a new employee. Consider the best way to deploy the human asset? Is the need short-term? The answer might be a contractor or temporary person. Is the need something where concentrated expertise is required? If so, the best solution may be to seek a consultant.

Finally, if the best way to satisfy the business need is with a full-time employee, look to hire a person who best satisfies the business need. And then do everything possible to maximize the asset.

The only reason to hire someone is to satisfy a business need. Clearly frame the business issue, and then determine the best way to address the need. Hiring new employees should not be the first thought when satisfying business needs.

The new economy necessitates hiring for the right reasons.

Chapter Five

Recruiting

Part One: Recruiting Philosophy

A good recruiting program is at the heart of every effective strategic staffing model. The new economy is forcing companies to look at recruiting differently. Recruiting can no longer be treated as a random act. Recruiting needs to be a habit, it needs to be a process, and it needs to be part of the strategic planning process to be successful.

In the new economy, there is the additional problem of having more candidates. There are far more people looking for jobs and responding to ads and postings. Attracting candidates is not the problem. Attracting *good* candidates is the problem and is getting more difficult. As a result, the approach to recruiting needs to change.

There are two categories of recruiting. The first is reactive recruiting. This is where the recruiting process does not begin until an open position is identified. This kicks off a flurry of activity and includes throwing a lot of time, effort and money at attracting candidates.

The second type of recruiting is proactive. Proactive recruiting is where the process of identifying and attracting new talent is ongoing. If talent is the lifeblood of the business, constant effort needs to be applied to attracting the best. Recruiting cannot be a random act.

This is a paradigm shift in thinking. Don't just recruit when there is an open position. Be proactive with all the recruiting activities. The hunt for top talent should be a never-ending process.

The goal of an effective recruiting program is to attract top players. It is not as simple as building a cadre of candidates. Top talent always has to be the focus.

To attract top players, the recruiting process needs to be geared toward building relationships. It takes a lot more than a clever ad or job posting to attract the "A" players. To attract the best, relationships need to be developed. It is critical to discover win-win deals if you are going to put a deal together.

Here is an example of the importance of relationships in recruiting. You are at a cocktail party and begin a conversation with a stranger. The third sentence out of your mouth is, *"Hey, do you want to work for my company?"* The person is going to think you are out of your mind. This is the equivalent of fly-by recruiting.

The opposite is to take time to establish a relationship. Learn a little about the person. Share some information about yourself. Once a mutual interest is established, it is possible to cultivate a relationship.

In translating this scenario to recruiting for a company the only difference is instead of a one-to-one relationship it is one-to-many. Effective recruiting necessitates cultivating relationships with many people simultaneously. This may seem to be a problem, but the great news is there is a solution. It is technology, and specifically, it is your website. This is the perfect medium to share information and begin the relationship building process.

The currency of the recruiting relationship is information. The person needs information about the company and position. You need information about the person, their background, behaviors and experience.

Using a website as part of the recruiting process provides a number of benefits. First, there is no limit to the amount of information that can be shared. And, there is no additional cost to adding more information. The web provides the opportunity to employ multiple delivery modes including print, audio and video. A well designed recruiting website provides the ability to establish relationships on a one-to-many basis. The foundation of an effective recruiting program includes a purpose-built website.

Quick note: The website does not need to be standalone. It can be the employment section of your company site.

Here are a couple of key ingredients in an effective recruiting website.

First, tell your story. Take as long as necessary. Consider including:

- The history of the company.
- Key company achievements.
- Financial achievements and successes.

- Employee benefits.
- The size of the company and the number of employees.
- The advantages of working for your company.
- And anything else the potential candidate might find useful.

Another key part of an effective recruiting website should be testimonials.

Most people think of testimonials strictly as a product endorsement. Testimonials don't need to be restricted to satisfied customers. What about satisfied employees? This is a great use of a testimonial?

The other beautiful thing about using a recruitment website is both audio and video are simple to incorporate. Consider including audio and video testimonials from satisfied employees. Have them share the reasons they came to work for the company. Have them share the reasons the company is a good place to work. Have them share successes. Think of all the possibilities.

Recruiting is no longer restricted to just the written word. A video tour of your plant can be powerful. The company's products and services can be explained in great detail via audio or video.

The philosophy of recruiting needs to change for the new economy. No longer is it effective to be reactive. The new goal is to attract the best people and begin a relationship. Use a recruiting website to take advantage of the wide variety of ways to deliver the message.

Chapter Five

Recruiting

Part Two: Recruitment-Planning

Like any other strategic business process, recruiting needs to be planned to be effective. Just as there are plans for sales, manufacturing, product development, and so forth, recruiting needs a plan.

There are four parts to a good, strategic recruiting plan.

Budget

There needs to be a budget covering all recruiting activities. Recruiting is not free. It takes time, effort and money. At the very minimum the budget should cover:

- How much is going to be spent
- When the money will be spent
- How it is going to be spent

A comprehensive recruiting plan always has a budget component.

Timing

The timing of recruiting affects planning. Some situations have the luxury of more lead-time. Examples of these include opening up a new plant, creating a new division, signing a new contract or just growing the company. In these situations, the business is going to need more human assets to service the growth. These situations generally afford enough lead-time to plan and execute the recruiting activities.

However, some situations don't allow the luxury of time. Replacing a key employee – like the earlier story when Mary walks into the office and resigns – is a situation where there is very little if any lead-time. In these situations there is little time to plan. As a result, some of the better sourcing techniques are not available due to the time constraints. The more lead-time available, the greater flexibility in where and how candidates can be recruited.

Timing contingencies must be built into the strategic recruiting plan.

Resources

It is important to determine, in advance, the resources available for recruiting activities. As mentioned previously, recruiting is not free. Not only does it require financial resources, it requires human resources as well. Someone has to do the work. Candidates don't miraculously appear, and even if they do, someone has to complete the screening and other tasks.

There needs to be a plan for where the assets come from and how they will be allocated. Are there internal resources? If so, do they have the capabilities, the breadth of knowledge and experience to handle the recruiting? Where is recruiting going to show up on their priority list? If it is not a priority, it is probably not going to get done.

If there are no internal resources, what external resources are available? Are there consultants or contractors available for use? If you choose to outsource the recruiting efforts, are the outsourced options qualified, available and affordable?

Part of the strategic recruiting plan has to be having the right resources identified and available.

Availability

Market conditions have a large impact on recruiting plans. Market conditions change over time. Analyze the current market conditions as part of the recruitment planning process. High unemployment dictates one course of action while low unemployment dictates a completely different strategy. There may be geographical concentrations of certain skill sets that affect the planning.

These are some of the issues that need to be considered under "availability". And these availability issues affect budgeting as well. More money, more time and more resources need to be budgeted when trying to hire people with rare skills. More money needs to be budgeted for relocations and for advertising if the geographical concentration of candidates is outside the immediate area.

To review, the four major planning issues of the recruiting plan are budget, timing, resources, and availability. Each component affects the other. They are interdependent.

There are two other issues to discuss before leaving the subject of recruitment planning. Each has a profound effect on the ability to recruit effectively.

The first issue is organizational reputation. This is how the organization is viewed in the marketplace. There are three possibilities. People in the marketplace whether that be local, national, international can react positively, negatively or have no reaction to the mention of the company.

Regardless of the specific reaction, there is an impact on recruiting. A bad reputation makes it much more difficult to attract top talent. A good reputation makes it much easier to recruit. No reputation is a hurdle that has to be overcome as well. More work and resources are needed to overcome a lack of reputation.

The final issue affecting recruitment planning is compensation. Although this book is not about compensation specifically, it needs to be mentioned. The way people are paid has a direct impact on the effort necessary to recruit. A generous pay package, at or above market, makes it is easier to recruit top talent. If the pay package is at or below market, it is more difficult to recruit top talent. That is a reality of the world.

How you choose to pay your employees is completely up to you. However, it is important to understand compensation practices impact the ability to recruit top talent.

Planning for recruiting has to be part of your staffing process.

Chapter Five

Recruiting

Part Three: Sourcing

This chapter is about sourcing. In other words, where can candidates be found? Sourcing options are only limited by imagination. There are an unlimited number of places to find candidates. In different situations, some sources work better than others. A number of options are discussed in this chapter.

Sourcing options can be broken into four major categories. The four categories are:

1. Personal
2. Offline
3. Outsourcing
4. Online

Each category is discussed below.

Personal Recruiting

The best way to think about identifying and attracting candidates from a personal perspective is to use the concept of Sphere of Influence—SOI. Think of all the people you have come into contact with in your career. Think of all the people you've worked with over the years. And, think of all the people you have come in contact with outside of work.

This is your SOI. It is sometimes called a personal network. The personal sphere of influence is the default place to start recruiting efforts.

Speaking of network, let's turn that into a verb. Networking should be an on-going effort. Always look for the opportunity to meet new people and participate in groups. They can be anything from alumni groups to professional organizations to social or religious groups. The goal is to continually expand your SOI through networking. Sometimes the easiest way to find good candidates is just to let your network know about open positions. Someone in the SOI will know someone else who is looking for a job, and it might work out perfect.

The power of a personal network can be multiplied exponentially if the concept is expanded and the network of all existing employees is accessed as well? This is where the concept of **employee referral** comes into play. An employee referral is where an existing employee is rewarded for referring candidates that eventually get hired.

A whole chapter could easily be devoted to employee referral programs. But here a couple of key points to help get started. First, every organization should have an employee referral program. Everyone benefits from a well-designed program. A number of studies that have shown the most loyal employees come through employee referrals. Employees should be rewarded either monetarily or some other way for referring a candidate that gets eventually hired by the organization.

Offline Recruiting

There are any number of offline ways to generate candidates for a business. The first option is advertising. Offline advertising falls into two categories. The first is traditional advertising. This includes newspapers, classifieds and magazines. The second category of offline advertising is nontraditional. This includes 3 X 5 cards, signs, flyers, and other creative, innovative ways to advertise an open position.

There are a few critical aspects to all advertising. In order of importance, advertising is affected by the following:

1. Medium
2. Headline
3. Copy
4. Call to action

Medium

The place chosen to run ads (the medium) has a greater impact on the results than everything else combined. In the right medium, meaning the right people are reading the message, there is the highest probability of attracting the right people. Try to determine where the target audience is most likely to see the ad. Determine what publications or blogs or web sources the target audience is reading. A good way to get this information is to ask existing employees what they read. Put as much effort into identifying the right medium for the ad as anything else.

Headline

Next in order of importance is the headline. The purpose of the headline is to grab attention and get the prospects to read the rest of the ad. If the headline does not catch their attention, then much of the effort will be wasted. The headline cannot be boring! It has to stand out from the crowd. "Come Join The Fastest Growing Accounting Firm In Cleveland" is much better than "Accountant Needed"

Copy

The third issue affecting advertising is the copy, the body of the ad. Enough information needs to be provided to keep interest. The copy needs to be interesting enough to get the person to the call to action.

Write ad copy from the candidate's perspective. Here is an example. Instead of "We are a 20 year-old company that is a leader in our industry" try "Imagine working for the leader in the industry who has posted 20 consecutive profitable years". The candidate is always interested in what is in it for them.

Call To Action

The final aspect of your advertising is the call to action. This is where it is clearly explained how the person should respond. This needs to be detailed and also simple to complete. Give people multiple ways to provide their information. Accept resumes via email, regular mail and fax. Don't limit the options.

Non-Traditional Advertising

Non-traditional advertising can really separate you from the crowd. Think of non-traditional advertising as anything the competition is not doing. The great thing about non-traditional advertising is it offers the opportunity to throw creativity, instead of money, at the recruiting.

3 x 5 cards, signs, and flyers are simple non-traditional forms of advertising. Don't limit yourself to just these options.

Here is how to best use creative advertising methods. Work backwards to determine where the target audience lives, works, congregates and socializes. Use this information to identify the best places to get their attention.

Next, figure out how to get their attention? When looking for young, active people, putting a 3 x 5 card up in a health club might be a good idea. When looking for a part-time person just to work a number of hours outside their house a day, you might put something up at the grocery store or at a senior center in the area.

These are a handful of non-traditional ideas.

Outsourced Recruiting

Outsourcing recruitment activities is a viable option. This is where a person or firm is hired to handle recruiting activities. Recruiting is not the easiest task in the world. As mentioned in the planning section, it does take time and effort to generate candidates. If you don't have the time or the expertise to recruit, think about outsourcing it.

There are two outsourcing options. The first option is using a recruiting firm. These are called recruiters/headhunters. This group can be broken into two groups. The first is contingency recruiters. These are firms that find candidates and are compensated only when a referred candidate is hired. The other group is the retained search firm. These organizations are contracted and paid up front regardless of the results. However, most often they do deliver results down the road. This option is usually reserved for higher-level employees.

The other outsourcing option is a consultant. There are a number of professional recruiters who manage project work. Some are human resource consultants or recruiting consultants who have their own business. This group can come in, working hourly or by the project, and complete specific recruiting activities. This service can range anywhere from just identifying names to managing the entire recruitment process.

Online Sourcing

The internet has become a prime tool in recruiting new employees. It can be an inexpensive way to attract high-quality candidates. The possible ways to use the internet to recruit are almost endless.

The primary option that also gets the most ink is the career sites. The largest of these are Monster.com, CareerBuilder.com and HotJobs.com. They offer a full package of services that apply to finding candidates.

The other job posting option, the one that happens to be my particular favorite, is specialty sites. These are job-posting sites that cater to a particular niche. For instance, in the technology world, there is a site called Dice.com that is strictly for programmers and computer specialists. Another example is a site called RestaurantJobs.com. As a restauranteur, you can find a chef or a server or a hostess on this site.

Most industries are going to have specialty job-posting websites. Doing a few minutes of research online should help identify the industry specific sites. As a final thought, check with associations covering your industry. Many of these have job-posting options or should be aware of the better options in your market.

In review, there are four categories of sourcing options. There is no one best choice. It will depend on circumstances. The real lesson here is to not limit efforts to just one or two sources. Try traditional as well as non-traditional sources to learn which work best for your business.

Chapter Five

Recruiting

Part Four: Social Media

It would be impossible to have a book on hiring and staffing in the new economy without talking about social media. The truth of the matter is social media is here to stay. And it can be a crucial tool in recruiting.

As of the writing of this book, there are more than 715 million accounts in just LinkedIn, Facebook, and Twitter. That isn't counting all the other social media sites that are out there. That is an awful lot of people.

Part of recruiting is going where the people are. Social media should be part of every recruiting strategy. It can be very cost effective.

The three primary tools for recruiting are going to be LinkedIn, Facebook, and Twitter. Let's go through each of those in order and show how each might be used as part of an effective recruiting program.

LinkedIn

LinkedIn has a heavy focus on business people. That is a great place to start. There are more business people involved with LinkedIn than any of the other social networking sites as of the writing of this book. It is not really geared towards consumers or the general public.

The first thing to do on LinkedIn is work your network. Let all the people who you are connected with know about any job openings. In addition, there is a paid option to post job openings on LinkedIn. It is a very moderate cost compared to some of the other options. It can be cost effective. Look into the paid option on LinkedIn and test for results.

Facebook

The next social media recruiting option is Facebook. Facebook is far and away the largest social media site with more than 500 million accounts. They are currently moving more towards business, and offer a number of options to help recruit candidates.

Here are a couple of ways to use Facebook. The first thing to do is search the Facebook Directory and look for groups. When looking for an accountant, see if there is a Facebook group for accountants. When looking for a sales rep, look for a Facebook group for sales rep, and so forth. This should provide a good starting point.

Next, it is possible to put a free job posting in the Facebook Marketplace. Follow all the rules discussed above under advertising to create the ad. This is a simple and inexpensive option to test.

In addition, there is a paid advertising option on Facebook. The beauty of Facebook ads is they can be targeted to specific groups or people who have certain keywords in their profile. And once again, armed with a good picture of the target person, Facebook ads can be a cost effective tool.

Twitter

The next social media recruiting option is Twitter. It is possible to tweet announcements of open positions. This is a great way to get the word out. Hopefully the tweets will get re-tweeted to an ever-expanding network.

Make sure to use the pound sign or the hash sign for categorizing in the tweets so people know that it is a job opening or recruiting. A lot of people use applications that will group the tweets according to those hash tags or pound signs.

Another way to use social media is for conducting research during the reference stage. This will be discussed in detail in the reference-checking chapter.

In today's world, social media has to be part of an effective recruiting program.

Chapter Six

Screening

Part One: Screening Overview

Once a group of top candidates are generated through all of the sourcing and recruiting techniques, the next step is screening. It is important to reduce the candidate pool to those that have the highest probability of succeeding on the job. In today's marketplace, more and more candidates are generated because there are more people looking for jobs. More people are crossing over from different industries and changing careers. As a result, screening candidates is becoming a much more difficult process.

In an ideal world, every candidate would be interviewed. That's the absolute best strategy. But practicality tells us that interviewing everybody isn't feasible given the time constraints. It is critical to only spend time with the highest quality candidates. This is why a screening process is necessary.

Most people go into the screening process with the goal of reducing the number of applicants to a more manageable number. It is a given that the number of applicants needs to be reduced but looking for reasons to eliminate people is the wrong approach. Step back from the process for a moment and look at the ultimate goal. The goal is to fill a position with a person who will satisfy the business need. Looking for reasons to eliminate people is in direct conflict with that goal.

The approach needs to change from **screening out to screening in**. On the surface this may seems counterintuitive but upon a closer look it is anything but. The goal is to hire someone and all efforts should be consistent with that goal. Every resume or application should be reviewed with the intent to find a reason to screen the person in. Don't look for reasons to throw the person out. Instead, find reason to throw them in.

This is a real philosophical switch. However it does have a number of advantages. First, more time is spent with each resume looking for positive information. It almost eliminates the "skimming" process. Second, this process forces all of the information in context. Reading between the lines and looking for the real story becomes standard practice.

But the numbers do have to be reduced.

Consistent with the new "screen in" philosophy, I developed a model to get the best information, screen in and reduce the numbers of applicants. It is called the "Higher Hurdle" model.

The Higher Hurdle model is a six-step process that continually raises the bar. At each point in the screening process the bar is raised by adding a new requirement or additional step. As the bar gets higher, the hurdle gets higher, and it makes it more difficult for people to get *into* the process. Remember: screen in, not out.

The Higher Hurdle model promotes getting more and better data throughout the screening process. This model is consistent with the principle that more data leads to better hiring decisions.

Here are the six steps of the Higher Hurdle model.

1. Sourcing Tactics and Copy

Sourcing was discussed in a previous chapter. Many of the things discussed fit with this model. Targeting the media where the ads are run and the job posted is the first step to the screening process. Posting ads in the right places, and using the right media, is an effective screening tactic. Targeting the right media leads to more targeted responses.

Write self-selecting copy. This means that the more specific the data in the copy, the better it should screen candidates.

If the ad reads, "I need someone who has designed rockets using the following principles..." hopefully the person who has worked in a convenience store is not going to apply. Make the copy as specific and detailed as possible to help the screening process.

2. Evaluation

There is a lot of data to deal with during the screening process. Screening decisions are made based on specific data points. The first data point to evaluate is the number of responses. The Higher Hurdles model is not really necessary if the recruiting only generated a small number of responses. However in the new economy it is often the case that the response is overwhelming. Based on a large response, the next decision is based on the available resources. Evaluate the internal resources. Choose a course of action based on the resources.

The resource availability is something that has to be evaluated to make good decisions about screening.

3. Additional Submissions

At the core of the Higher Hurdle model is getting more information at each step. Typically a resume or application is received from a candidate. In many cases, that's not a whole lot of information. A good way to get more data is have them submit additional information. When looking for graphic artists, get samples of the person's work.

For a programmer or an engineer, have them submit a program or engineering plan they created. These additional submissions add much more data to help make the screening decision.

In addition to work samples, it is helpful to ask for written responses to questions. Develop a set of standard questions that relate to your business: *"The three biggest issues that we're facing in our organization right now are A, B, and C. Please write a response to what your experience has been handling those particular issues."*

Now, in addition to the resume, and/or application, you've got written samples. Use this information to evaluate writing skills. The responses to written questions are an opportunity to evaluate their approach to problem solving, their ability to research and to put ideas together. Each additional submission provides more data. Remember, more data leads to better decisions.

4. Read Resumes

In the next chapter reading resumes will be covered in great detail. Here is how reading resumes fits into the higher hurdles model. The Higher Hurdles model suggests adding additional levels when reading resumes. If there are six requirements for the position, most people read the resume looking for the two most critical requirements. Assuming 50 applicants, this might result in the number of applicants screened in to 20. But 20 is still too large a number to manage. The next step is to add a third requirement. Now the number of screened in is reduced to 6 or 7.

Adding requirements—remember the Higher Hurdles model— to the resume-reading process results in better data and spending interview time with the highest potential applicants.

Remember, in the next chapter, I'll go through some very detailed information about how to read resumes.

5. Using Quantitative Assessment Tools

Testing tools can be a positive part of the selection process. There is a whole array assessment tools in the market. Testing is a self-contained subject and is covered in a chapter later in the book.

As part of the Higher Hurdle model adding testing and assessments to the screening process is one more hurdle to gain more information.

6. Phone Screen

Once again, in a following chapter there is a complete discussion covering phone screens. The phone screen contributes to the Higher Hurdles model by presenting an opportunity to ask specific questions directly to the applicants. As few as four to six prepared questions can add a tremendous amount of data and help screen in.

Remember, the whole purpose of screening process is to make one decision. That decision is which applicants are going to go to the next step. The next step is the face-to-face interview. That's the purpose of screening.

Once again, let's review the six steps of the Higher Hurdles model:

1. Sourcing tactics and copy
2. Evaluation of responses and resources
3. Additional submissions
4. Read resumes
5. Conduct assessments or testing
6. Conducting a phone screen.

Chapter Six

Screening

Part Two: Reading Resumes

Reading resumes effectively is critical to a successful staffing program. Unfortunately, most people have never been taught how to get the most information from a resume. Too often people read a resume like any other document and that is not effective. Here is a step-by-step process to get the most value from every resume read.

Here are two important thoughts before the six-step resume screening process is revealed. First, it is important to understand what a resume represents. There are lots of myths, and misinformation about resumes. A resume is a marketing document. It's a document a person uses to market their background and experience. And marketing documents generally don't contain a lot of negatives.

The popular press contends that resumes are littered with lies and misinformation. This is not true. My experience shows less than 10% of resumes have outright lies. Are there omissions? Sure, there are omissions. Do people play up the best and downplay the worst? Of course they do. It's a marketing document. However, I just don't believe outright lying happens anywhere near as often as some might profess.

Keep in mind; a resume is a marketing document.

The second thought to remember is to screen in, not screen out. Most people, when confronted with a large number of resumes, are looking for reasons to eliminate. But as I mentioned earlier, screening out is the opposite of the goal to hire someone. Screen in. Find a reason to throw the person in each time a resume is read.

Now the bad news ... by using the new screen in model it takes longer with each resume. To really read and study the document takes time. There is no way to effectively review a resume in 10 seconds and do a quality job.

The good news is the reward for taking a little longer is much better data and that makes the screening decision easier and more accurate.

Here are the six steps to use when screening resumes.

1. Identify The Requirements

The list of critical hiring requirements, which are discussed in great detail in an upcoming chapter, includes all of the knowledge, skills and behaviors necessary for the particular position. The first step in screening is to review this list.

Some of the requirements should be evident on a resume. Some don't show up on a resume at all. For instance, a particular programming language should be simple to identify on the resume. If the hiring requirement is for a person who knows how to utilize a certain type of machinery, that skill should show up on a resume.

However, some of the behaviors are not as easy to identify from the resume. Initiative, flexibility and reliability are much more difficult to glean from the resume.

The solution is to go through the list of hiring requirements and identify those that should be evident on the resume. Use that subset of hiring requirements as the target list for screening the resumes.

2. Read Resumes in Correct Chronological Order

Resumes should be read starting at the beginning of the person's career and working to the present. In most cases, specifically in North America, resumes are written in reverse chronological order. They start with the person's most recent experience and back towards the beginning of their career. Reading resumes in correct chronological order, from back to front and bottom to top, is very important because of the next two steps.

3. Identify Trends and Patterns

The resume should reveal trends and patterns over time. It's very difficult to identify trends and patterns working in reverse chronological order. Look to see if the person does things consistently. Look for evidence of growth. Look for learning and picking up new skills. See if the person does things better, faster and to a higher quality level over time. Screen for trends and patterns.

4. Look For Accomplishments

Look for trends and patterns of accomplishments. The accomplishments should be the same or similar to those the person needs to deliver on your job. If the job requires resolving customer problems, look for trends and patterns of how they've resolved customer problems and concerns over time.

If troubleshooting financial documents is required on the job, try to find trends and patterns where they've worked with financial documents. If the job requires testing and debugging computer programs, find trends and patterns of how they have tested and debugged computer programs. Patterns of accomplishment, growth and learning should be evident.

There is a key distinction when looking for accomplishments. Be certain to find accomplishments and not responsibilities. This is a key distinction because responsibilities only indicate what the person was *supposed* to do. People are not hired to be responsible for things. People are hired to deliver results. Many resumes are written around responsibilities. This makes it important to read between the lines and search for the actual accomplishments.

If the resume states they were responsible for managing the accounts receivables, look to determine how well this was accomplished. Repeat this for all of the requirements.

5. Use the scoreboard

It is important to grade and track each resume. The simplest of all systems is a scoreboard. Create a 2-column board with the left-hand column labeled with a plus. Label the right-hand column with a minus.

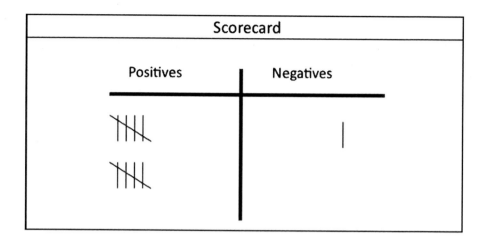

Work through the resume in correct chronological order and for each positive accomplishment place a mark on the positive side. If there's something missing, or there is negative accomplishment, place a mark on the negative side.

The beauty of this system is it makes it very difficult to skim a resume. It forces the reader to take sufficient time, pay attention and read between the lines. The reader has to analyze the data on the resume.

This also prevents the common problem of a single negative overly influencing the process. Too often, if the first thing seen on the resume is negative—if they went to the wrong school for instance, the resume is "screened out". However by using the scoreboard, the person only receives a mark on the negative side. The rest of the information still has to be reviewed. The next fifteen accomplishments might be positive. The scoreboard helps avoid the screening-out disease.

6. Only Screen Five Resumes Per Session

Screening resumes is difficult work. It requires concentration and focus. Trying to screen 100 responses to an ad or a posting is a daunting task.

Too often concentration wanes by the time the tenth document is reached. The rest of the resumes don't receive the same consideration. Try to limit each session to no more than five resumes.

Final Thoughts On Screening Resumes

Here are a couple of final thoughts about resumes. First, discount the style of the resume. Don't place too much emphasis on how the resume looks. Don't worry if it is one page or two pages. Don't worry if it is organized functionally or chronologically. Don't ignore style issues but don't give them too much credit.

In the old model of screening out, a four-page resume is usually screened out immediately. The length alone is a reason to eliminate the resume. In the screen-in model, a four-page resume with clear, concise, positive data can be a real gem.

There is certainly an alternative argument. It can be argued a resume is an example of how a person sells. However, the bottom line is almost no one knows how to write a resume. Much of the popular literature on how to write a resume is not very good. It is difficult to hold people accountable for the style of their resume. After all, you are not hiring people to write resumes. People are hired to deliver accomplishments so look for that information.

The last thought on resumes is about cover letters. There's a lot of controversy about cover letters. My philosophy is to read the cover letter last. Read the cover letter after completing the scoreboard and only if there is interest. It's the last activity, not the first.

There are a couple of points to pay attention to when reading the cover letter. First, look for writing skills. The cover letter is certainly an example of the person's writing. Don't give it too much weight but pay attention. Also, look for customization. Look to see if the cover letter resembles a boilerplate document, or if it is written for the particular position and organization?

Here is a review of the key principles of reading resumes. Number one, screen in, not out. Then go through the six-step process to get the information necessary to screen the resumes. The goal is to decide which applicants will continue to the next step in the hiring process.

Chapter Six

Screening

Part Three: Phone Screen

The last step of the Higher Hurdles screening model was a phone screen. The purpose of the phone screen is to add more data and determine whether or not to proceed to the next step. Each of the other screening steps led to the best applicants, but more data is necessary before making the decision to conduct live interviews.

The phone screen is conducted before the decision to schedule a face-to-face interview. There are two options in how to conduct the phone screen. The first is option is called the vertical option. The vertical option requires choosing one critical requirement to explore. This is usually the most important requirement. For a sales person the choice might be sales skills. It would be the prime programming language for a computer programmer.

After choosing the requirement, develop one question for each timeframe in a person's background. Generate four to six questions covering four to six timeframes. This results in a vertical slice through the person's background where more information about one critical requirement is identified. View this as a tall, narrow journey through the person's background.

The second phone screen option is the horizontal option. With this option, the focus is on the person's most recent job. Develop one question for each of the critical requirements as it relates to their most recent job. Once again, there will be four to six questions. This horizontal slice through the person's background results in more data. This is thin, wide exploration of the person's background.

Both options are equally effective. Choose the option that makes the most sense for your situation. In either case, the phone screen only needs to take 10 to 15-minutes. This small investment in time pays great dividends in the amount of information available to make the screening decision.

Here is the opening script I've used for 20-plus years to open every phone screen:

"Hello. This Barry Shamis with Selecting Winners, and I'm calling about the resume that we received. I was wondering if this was a good time to spend ten or fifteen minutes of your time? We are at the stage where we are learning a little bit more about a few of the applicants, and I wanted to ask you a few questions."

That's all that is necessary to set the stage for the phone screen.

Here is one final note regarding phone screens. This is an opportunity to cover some logistical information before investing time in a face-to-face interview.

There may be questions regarding salary. The most you can pay for the job is $50,000 a year and the applicant is making $100,000. This should be covered in the phone screen before either side has invested a whole lot of time in the process.

A discussion of travel requirements might be warranted if the job involves a lot of travel. Relocation can be discussed during the phone screen.

The purpose of the phone screen is to gather more data and decide if this person will be invited to the next step in the process.

Chapter Six

Screening

Part Four: Video Screening

Video screening is a new technology that can be applied to the screening process. The technology for video screening has come a long way. Video conferencing has been around for more than 15 years. It used to be necessary to go to a conferencing center in a major city to take advantage of the technology. Today, there are tools including Skype, GoToMeeting, WebEx and other similar tools that can be used right from your desk and computer.

There are two ways to take advantage of video technology when screening applicants. The first is as an actual screening tool. There are services available that create a video of the applicant. The person is presented with a series of questions. The responses are recorded on video and then made available to the organization. The video can be reviewed as needed and by multiple people.

The second use of video is actual "face-to-screen" interviews. This is where you get in front of a computer, and with the candidate in front of their computer, have a real-time videoconference. This provides the opportunity to conduct a phone screen or short interview live in a face-to-screen environment.

There are advantages and disadvantages to video screening. One of the advantages is the process is inexpensive. It's a whole lot cheaper than getting on an airplane. Also, it saves time. There is the opportunity to get more data including the visual feedback of talking to the person live.

The disadvantages include adding to the stress of the candidate. There's something about being live on video, with a camera, that elevates a candidate's stress level. Anything that increases a candidate's anxiety level lowers the quality of data.

Another disadvantage is dealing with technology glitches. Even with super high-speed Internet connections, occasional problems arise with the technology. Sometimes there are time delays.

For years, I advised against using video primarily because of the technology. It was a very awkward environment. But as the technology has improved— and it's really outstanding today — I am in favor of using video screening. The best option is video screening where a live questions and answer is conducted with the candidate. It is possible to get so much more data when talking to the person live.

In the new economy, video screening is an option that should be explored.

Chapter Seven

Testing & Assessment

Pre-employment testing and assessment tools are an option that can be considered for your staffing process. There is a lot of controversy in the marketplace about testing. As economic conditions have changed, testing has become more popular. Companies have reacted to the large number of applicants by using testing.

Here is a discussion of the subject to help make informed decisions about whether or not to incorporate assessments into the staffing process.

Testing or assessment tools are quantitative instruments designed to identify behavior and skills information about perspective candidates. The terms "tests" and "assessments" are interchangeable and we will use the term "tests" for the remainder of the chapter.

First thing to understand is there are a number of different types and categories of tests. The first category is an assessment center. Assessment centers are a whole series of instruments, tests and simulations that candidates need to complete. They can run for multiple days. They are very comprehensive and also very effective. The problem is they are also very, very expensive and hard to create. Most small businesses are not going to use assessment centers. It is important to know that assessment centers are an option.

The next category is tests that measure cognitive ability. These instruments test for things like the ability to learn, reasoning and reading comprehension.

The next type of test is integrity tests. These measure traits including honesty, dependability, reliability, pro-social behavior, and similar issues.

Next, there are job knowledge tests. These test for very specific knowledges including things like accounting knowledge or programming knowledge. Many of these tools are designed for specific industries and professions.

The largest and widest category of tests is personality tests. These test for traits relating to behavior at work. This can include service-orientation, openness, optimism, stress tolerance, and other similar traits.

Another category of tests is physical ability tests, which is really self-explanatory. Examples of this category include strength or balance or speed tests when those are job-related issues.

There are a number of considerations when deciding whether to incorporate tests into your selection process. The first is to make certain of the quality of the test you choose. All legitimate, pre-employment tests have two characteristics that measure of their effectiveness. The two measures are reliability and validity. If you are going to purchase any tests, these are numbers that absolutely need to be discussed with the vendors. Be certain to receive documentation of the numbers.

Reliability is a measure of the consistency of test results. In simple terms, if you test me today and test me a year from now, the test results should be the same. Tests should have a high reliability number.

Validity measures the accuracy of the test. A simple way of thinking about this is the higher the score, the better the employee should be. The best employees should score the highest on the test.

Make certain to get information about reliability and validity scores before considering any tool. These are standard measures and every vendor should provide this information. Don't consider any tool where this information is not provided.

Pre-employment testing makes more sense in certain positions. Make sure there is sufficient value from any investment in testing tools.

The first example of when testing contributes value is volume positions. If there are 35 customer service people in the organization, it may make sense to test for that particular position. There should be many examples of top performing employees to use as a benchmark.

The other example of good use of testing is when the test is proven to predict specific job requirements. Look for a strength test if the job requires lifting 50 pounds. The test is a good measure of a specific job requirement.

No discussion of testing and assessment is complete without looking at the legal considerations. First, let me throw in this disclaimer. I am not an attorney, and I am not dispensing legal information. It is important to understand that testing is a legal minefield. There is lots of pending litigation as it relates to testing and how companies use testing. Be very careful when using testing. Always consult outside counsel before incorporating testing into the staffing process. Make sure to get the stamp of approval that no laws are being violated. This is both a good idea and a good investment.

By all means, do not take the vendor's word for the legality of the instrument. If the vendor says, *"Oh sure, this is a legal and reliable instrument,"* don't take their word for it. Have legal counsel review the information provided by the vendor.

Once the decision is made to use testing, there are a couple of implementation issues. First, make certain the people chosen to administer or the people delivering the tests are well trained. It is critical they've gone through training and know what they are doing.

Second, keep accurate records. Every test needs to be scored and records kept on every person that goes through the process. This is an absolute legal requirement to keep the testing program legal.

Third, be consistent. Be very consistent in all procedures when it comes to testing. Everyone should be tested under the same conditions and at the same point in the process.

Finally, continuously evaluate the effectiveness of the testing for both reliability and validity. Are the people who are scoring high on the tests turning out to be top performers? If not, there is a problem.

Here is one final thought on testing. Most people see testing as a shortcut. It is absolutely not a shortcut. It can add data to the pot to help make better hiring decisions. But it is only effective when it is part of an integrated selection system.

Chapter Eight

Achievement-based Profile

It is absolutely impossible to hire good employees without a clear description of the successful person. That sounds so basic and so simple. But the number one reason companies make more hiring mistakes than necessary is not having a clear, specific profile of the successful person.

Most interviewers go into the interview thinking; *"I'll know it when I see it"*. It is human nature to feel confident about figuring out people. Unfortunately, we can't. A clear and concise profile of the successful person is the tool that directs the activities to the most critical data.

The reason to hire is to satisfy a business need. The person hired needs to deliver specific results and behave in a specific way to successfully satisfy the business need. To hire effectively, it is necessary to identify and record both these outcomes and behaviors in a profile.

As part of my **Selecting Winners** system, we created the Achievement-based Profile (AP). The AP is a template of the successful person. The template is used to drive all the data gathering activities and as an evaluation matrix to evaluate each of the candidates. It is the roadmap used throughout the selection process.

The Achievement-based Profile cannot be fuzzy. A roadmap that is not perfectly clear leads to missing the target when hiring. There is an important distinction to make about the AP. An Achievement-based Profile is not a job description.

Most organizations use the job description to drive the hiring process. But the job description is not the right document to use in the hiring process. Job descriptions are important. They serve a legal purpose. However, a job description is a picture of a job and the goal of the hiring process is not to hire a job.

The goal is to hire a person.

Creating a picture of a job is not the right answer. The tool needed to hire great employees is a template of a successful person. The Achievement-based Profile does exactly that. The job description is a useful tool in creating the Achievement-based Profile, but it is not the document to drive the hiring process. There is a large distinction between the AP and a job description.

There are two parts to the Achievement-based Profile. The first half is a list of expected outcomes. The reason to hire a new employee is to satisfy a business need. The person has to deliver specific results in order to satisfy the business need. These specific results are expected outcomes. The definition of a successful employee is the person that accomplishes the most.

In building the list of expected outcomes, the best way to begin is to break the job into three time periods: short, medium, and long-term. Next, put specific numbers next to the time frames. What is a reasonable short-term period where the person can deliver results to the organization? That is the short-term time frame.

The time frames are different depending upon the job. Short-term may be one week for an administrative position but could be as long as six months for a research engineer.

After determining the short-term period for the position, decide on the time frame for both medium-term and long-term? Don't stress over the actual numbers. The goal is to break a very large, difficult job into a series of smaller more manageable pieces.

With the time frames identified, the next step is to identify the expected outcomes for each period. This is a list of the specific results the person has to deliver to satisfy the business need and earn the label of success.

Here is a visualization exercise to help in generating the list of expected outcomes. Project to the end of the short-term time frame and ask; "What must the person have delivered by this time to earn the label of success?" Repeat the process for both medium-term and long-term. The result is a list of everything the person needs to deliver. This list is the perfect representation of your expected outcomes.

Another technique to help with this exercise is to project to the end of the time period and ask, *"What has to happen to make me happy?"* A successful employee delivers results that bring a smile to your face. Review the list of expected outcomes and see if it passes the "happiness test".

The key rule when listing expected outcomes is to make certain each is specific and measurable. This is another real distinction from the typical job description. A specific outcome leaves no doubt as to your expectation. Instead of, "Responsible for sales in the XYZ territory" a specific outcomes reads, "By the end of 90 days they will have generated $100,000 in sales". That outcome is specific, measurable and time bound.

There are two reasons the expected outcomes must be specific, measurable and time bound. First, success cannot be quantified without specific measures. Second, it is very difficult to communicate expectations to a new employee if they are not specific, measurable and time bound. A detailed list of expected outcomes not only makes it easier to choose good employees but it makes it easier to manage them as well.

The acid test for the expected outcomes half of the AP is success. The list of short, medium, and long-term expected outcomes is the definition of success.

The second half of the AP is a list of the critical requirements necessary to deliver the expected outcomes. There are two types of critical requirements. The first, larger category of requirements is job requirements. These are all the requirements a person has to possess to be successful on the job. The second category is actually a subset of the first. The second category is the hiring requirements.

The difference between job requirements and hiring requirements is job requirements include all the hiring requirements plus the knowledge, skills and abilities you are willing to train.

Product knowledge is an example of a job requirement that might not be a hiring requirement. Product knowledge is certainly a job requirement. It would be difficult to be successful without product knowledge. However, product knowledge is not a hiring requirement if you are willing to train it on the job. Keep this distinction in mind, as the requirements on the AP are all hiring requirements.

Another differentiator that applies to hiring requirements is the distinction between "musts" and "wants". "Musts" are hiring requirements that have to be present. The person will not be hired if a "must" requirement is missing. "Wants" are nice to have but do not disqualify the person if missing. Only the "must" hiring requirements are included on the AP.

The critical hiring requirements on your AP are used to evaluate the candidate and determine whether or not they will be hired.

There are three categories of critical hiring requirements. They are knowledge, skills, and behaviors. Let's look at each individually.

Knowledge

Knowledge is defined as what the person must know to successfully deliver the expected outcomes. A candidate for an accounting position has to know the general principles of accounting to be hired. A programmer, who has to program in C++ language, has to know C++ language to be hired.

To determine the list of knowledge requirements ask the question, "What does the person need to know to successfully deliver the expected outcomes?"

Skills

The second category of hiring requirements is skills. Skills are defined by identifying what the person must do to successfully deliver the expected outcomes. Think about the skills the person has to apply to the tasks of the job. For a sales position, the person has to have the skill to manage sales campaigns and close sales deals. A programmer needs to write clear legible technical documentation to successful deliver the required expected outcomes. A civil engineering position might require surveying skills.

Often with entry-level positions you are willing to train many of the job requirements. This goes back to the "must" versus the "want" hiring requirement. Any skill expected of the person day one, should be included on the hiring requirements list. Examples of these skills may include certain technical skills, writing skills and the ability to follow directions.

Behaviors

The third category of hiring requirements is behaviors. Behavior simply means how the person handles the tasks and situations to successfully deliver the expected outcomes. Think of behavior requirements as the "how" part of performance.

The list of behavior requirements is going to describe how the outcomes of the job need to be delivered. The person that does the right things but does those things in a way inconsistent with success in the organization is not going to be labeled successful. The salesperson who delivers great revenue but lies, cheats, and steals to close the deals, does not earn the label of being successful.

Here are some samples of behaviors that might be necessary:

- Considers multiple option before choosing the best (Judgment)
- Managing multiple projects simultaneously (Flexibility)
- Takes independent, unprompted action (Initiative)
- Influences individuals and groups toward a common goal (Leadership)

Behavior is all about how they act and react to the tasks while delivering the results.

There are two clarifications to consider when it comes to job-related behaviors. The first is that business models dictate style. The way a company does business, their business model, requires their employees to behave a certain way. This means the company dictates a part of a person's behavior on the job.

A good example of this principle is how a company approaches risk. High-risk organizations require employees to behave in a way where they take good calculated risks in the course of doing their job. A very conservative business requires employees to behave differently. In this company, someone who takes a lot of calculated risks will not be successful. Business models dictate style.

Here is a story to illustrate the point. A company hires a top performer from a direct competitor. The person comes into the organization and fails. The person certainly didn't get stupid overnight. More likely, the behavior necessary for success in the competitor's environment was different than the behavior necessary for success at the new company.

Here is another example. At company A, everything is done in small team groups. At company B, people operate as individuals running their own show. Hiring a person from company A to company B, or the reverse, probably leads to a hiring mistake.

Business models dictate style. This is something that needs to be researched during the interview.

The second clarification regarding job-related behavior deals with soft skills. Culture, fit, chemistry and style are all examples of soft skills that pertain to hiring. They are critical issues but when it comes to interviewing for them, the process is not clear. The first problem with these terms is they are labels and open to interpretation. More often then not, they introduce ambiguity instead of clarity.

The way to successfully interview and screen for soft skills is to translate them into behaviors.

The **magic sentence** is a tool created in our **Selecting Winners** model. It is used to translate labels like culture, fit, style and chemistry into behaviors. The magic sentence is as follows:

"How does someone with _____ behave?"

To define the term team player, ask the question, *"How does someone who is a team player behave?"*

The answer might be, *"They share ideas with other people. They contribute to team efforts. They put the team's goal ahead of their own."* Those are specific behaviors that can be explored in the interview by using effective questions.

To define the term creativity, ask the question, *"How does someone who is creative behave?"*

The answer might be, *"The person looks for unique and innovative solutions to difficult problems."* Once again, that is a specific behavior that can be explored in the interview.

It is important to stay away from ambiguous terms like culture, fit and chemistry. Ambiguity is the enemy in the selection process. Translate those ambiguous labels into behavior using the magic sentence and your AP becomes much more effective.

Each of the hiring requirements should consist of a label (flexibility) and the behavioral definition of the label (handles multiple projects simultaneously). Adding the definition to the label eliminates any ambiguity and points directly to the data needed in the interview.

Let's review. A very clear template of the successful person is necessary. There are two pieces to the Achievement-based Profile template. The first half is the expected, performance outcomes. This is a list of what the person needs to accomplish and the results that need to be delivered for the person to earn the label of success. It includes short, medium, and-long term expected outcomes. The outcomes need to be specific, measurable, and time bound.

The second half of the Achievement-based Profile template is a list of the critical hiring requirements. Each hiring requirement is a "must". They fall into three categories. Knowledge is what the person must know to successfully deliver the outcomes. Skills are what the person must do to successfully deliver the outcomes. Behaviors are how the person handles the tasks and situations to successfully deliver the expected outcomes. Each hiring requirement has a label and a behavioral definition.

Think of the first half of the AP as the "what" the person has to do and the second half as the "how" the person needs to behave.

A fully comprehensive Achievement-based Profile is the template that drives all hiring decisions. A blank AP form is included in the appendix.

Chapter Nine

The Behavioral Model

It is important to have a guiding principle when hiring new employees. In this chapter I am going to share the guiding principle that my **Selecting Winners** clients have used successfully for more than 30 years.

The goal when choosing an employee is to **predict success on the job**. Success means delivering the expected outcomes in the right way to satisfy the business need. The goal of hiring is not to figure people out.

With the goal to predict success on the job, it is important to understand the components of a job. A job boils down to a series of tasks that need to be completed and a series of situations that need to be handled. That is a job in its simplest form. Of course each job has different tasks and situations.

Once a person is on the job, they act and react to the tasks and situations. This is their behavior. Behavior is defined as how the person handles the tasks and situation of a job.

People earn labels based on how they behave on the job. The successful person is the person who deals effectively with the tasks and handles the situations appropriately. The person earns the labels of success when they do the right things the right way, and delivers the desired outcome.

Predict Success ⇨ Tasks & Situations ⇨ Behavior ⇨ Earn Success Label

Going back to the beginning, the purpose is to predict success on the job. A job consists of tasks and situations. Success is defined as applying the correct behavior to the tasks and situations.

As a result, the strategy in the interview needs to be to predict the person's behavior. Not get in their head and figure them out. Just predict how the person will handle the tasks and situations of the job.

Hiring decisions are simple when you know how the person will behave.

The great news is there is a statistical model that makes predicting behavior very simple. The model is called **The Behavioral Model**. This model has been around for many years and there is a wealth of data supporting it.

The Behavioral Model in its simplest form says:

Past Behavior Predicts Future Behavior

Here is how the behavioral model works. Put a person in a situation, with a given set of circumstances, they act or react a certain way. Put the person in the same or similar set of circumstances in the future, they act or react the same way. This is true to a stunningly high degree of reliability. The social scientists claim on average, people repeat behavior 88% of the time.

We are creatures of habit.

The way a person handles stress is a good example. Some people exercise. Some people drink. Some people cry. However they handle stress, they tend to do it the same way every single time. Behavioral patterns are very powerful predictors. Using the Behavioral Model predicting how a person will handle stressful situations on our job is as simple finding out how they handled similar situations in the past.

The Behavioral Model acts as the guiding principle for the selection model because it is so incredibly accurate. And, there are opportunities to add to the accuracy.

Documenting past behavior is the easiest and most accurate method to predict job behavior. Instead of trying to "figure people out", we will ask questions to determine how the person has handled the same or similar tasks and situations in the past.

Don't try to get inside people's heads and play amateur psychologist. This is easier said than done. We all want to believe we can "read" other people. But why even try? No matter how good we might believe we are at reading people, it is impossible to approach the accuracy of the behavioral model.

Simply chronicle how they behaved in the same or similar situation to those they will face on your job, and trust that the Behavioral Model works. The odds are overwhelming the person will repeat the behavior and act the same way on your job.

Here is an example in my company. We don't allow our salespeople to discount the price of our services. I have to know how a prospective salesperson is going to behave in a situation where they get pushback on price. It is a situation they are likely to face. How the person has handled this situation in the past is the best indicator of how they will handle the situation when working for me. If they handle it one way, they will be successful. If they handle it a different way, they will be unsuccessful.

In the course of interviewing sales candidates, I get multiple examples of how they dealt with price objections in past sales cycles. The data almost always points to a very consistent behavioral pattern.

The Behavioral Model is the single best statistical predictor of future behavior. As a result, all of the data gathering efforts in the selection process are designed to chronicle the person's past behavior.

Chapter Ten

Interview Questions

Part One: Characteristics of Effective Questions

Interview questions are the single most important component of an effective selection process. The only type of questions that should be asked in an interview is effective questions. To fully understand that statement, it is important to define the term **effective question**.

An effective question is any question that gets information that helps predict success. As was discussed in the previous chapter, past behavior predicts future behavior. The important data from the interview is the person's past behavior. Effective questions are questions that get information and data about past behavior.

Effective interview questions have four characteristics.

- Easy to answer
- Only one answer
- Specific planned purpose
- Job related

Easy To Answer

Don't ask hard questions, difficult questions, and multi-part questions. Any question that requires the candidate to think increases anxiety and lowers the quality of data.

Although this may sound counterintuitive, it is true. The questions asked in the interview need to be so simple that the candidate doesn't need to think about the answer. The person is simply sharing how they handled situations and tasks in the past and should not have to think about those answers. Tough, difficult questions put the candidate under pressure, increase anxiety and lower the quality of data received. It doesn't help in any way, shape, or form to ask difficult questions.

Only One Answer

The second characteristic of effective questions is they have only one answer. Every question asked in an interview should have only one answer. By definition, this means only closed-ended questions should be asked. The definition of a closed-ended question is any question that has only one answer.

Let me show some examples before you get up in arms. A typical interview question is, "Tell me about dealing with deadlines". This is an open-ended question. The candidate has the option of answering with any number of responses. There is no single answer that is correct. The closed-ended version of this question is, *"How did you handle the budget deadline on the ABC project?"* With this question, there is only one correct answer. The answer is what the person did in that specific situation.

The result of closed-ended questions is specific, behavioral data about how the person handled a deadline. This information is then used to predict future behavior.

There are four problems with open-ended questions.

1. Open-ended questions put the candidate under pressure. In response to an open-ended question the person thinks, *"Oh my, what are they looking for?"* Trying to figure out what the interviewer is looking for creates increased stress. As the person's anxiety level goes up, the quality of data goes down. The goal is to put the person at ease, not create stress.
2. Opened-ended questions provide an opportunity for the person to give the "book answer". Too often the person tries to figure out what the interviewer is looking for and gives that answer. This is not good data and does not help predict future behavior.
3. There is no statistical correlation between the answer the person gives to an open-ended question and future behavior. Open-ended

questions are fairy tales with no basis in fact. The answer leaves you guessing what the person will actually do in the future. A closed-ended question about their behavior results in a behavioral answer.
4. Open-ended questions cause loss of control of the interview. Controlling the interview will be covered in great detail in a later chapter however controlling the interview means controlling the agenda. Are you getting the data needed or getting the data the candidate chooses to share? These may no be the same sets of data.

As soon as an open-ended question is asked, the candidate controls the agenda and the interviewer has lost control of the interview.

Stay away from open-ended questions and keep make certain each questions has only one answer.

Specific Planned Purpose

The third characteristic of effective questions is they have specific, planned purpose. Every question should be asked for a reason. The reason to ask all questions is the same – **You need a piece of data.**

The AP detailed all the information needed to make a good hiring decision. There are a number of expected outcomes and a number of critical hiring requirements. For each requirement, data needs to be gathered. Questions are designed and asked to get this specific information.

Specific information is needed and effective questions should be designed to get the specific piece of information. Interviewing is not just a fishing expedition.

Job Related

The fourth characteristic of effective questions is they are job related. Stay out of the candidate's personal life. The goal is to predict how the person will handle the situations on this job. The best way to get there is to explore how they handled similar situations in the past. This has nothing to do with their personal life.

One reason to avoid a candidate's personal life is to avoid the legal liabilities. There are a variety of areas that are "off limits" in a person's personal life. It is not worth the trouble to list them here. The most important reason to avoid questions regarding personal life is there is no functional business reason to do so. Spend the time exploring work related experiences and behavior. Keep the questions job related by finding out how they handled the same or similar situations to those they will face on your job.

To review, the only types of questions to ask in an interview are **effective questions**. Effective questions have four characteristics. They are easy to answer, have only one answer, have specific planned purpose and are job related.

Chapter Ten

Interview Questions

Part Two: Types of Effective Questions

There are six types of questions that should be asked in interviews. Questions not in these categories should be avoided.

1. Factual Questions

The first type of effective interview question is factual questions. Factual questions are defined as any question that requires an answer with a discreet piece of information. *How many new accounts did you open up last year? What accounting software do you use? How many people worked on that project? How long did it take to complete that project?*

The answer to every one of those questions is a simple, discreet fact. Somewhere along the line we got way off base when asking questions. For some reason we stopped asking straightforward direct questions. In an interview, most of the questions should be simple straightforward factual questions that are simple to answer and require a short discreet answer.

2. Action Questions

The second type of effective interview question is action questions. Action questions require the person to describe past behavior. The answer has to be how the person completed tasks and dealt with situations. Remember, the goal is to chronicle a person's past behavior. The simplest, easiest way to do that is to ask how they handled tasks and situations. Here are some examples:

For a salesperson: *"How did you build this year's territory management plan?"*
For an engineer: *"How did you put your project plan together?"*
For a management candidate: *"How did you staff your department?"*
For a clerical candidate: *"How did you put the filing system in place?"*

These are all questions that require the person to describe behavior. They are very simple questions to answer but provide great information that helps predict future behavior.

3. Candidate Specific Questions

The third type of effective interview question is candidate specific questions. These are questions tailored to the specific person and the specific situation. They are the opposite of general, generic questions.

There are books with hundreds of interview questions. The problem with the questions in these books is the general inference is to ask everyone the same questions. If you are going to ask everyone the same questions, the questions have to be general, generic questions. Questions like, *"How do you deal with deadlines?"* and *"Tell me about a time you solved a customer problem"* are examples of general, generic questions. General questions cause loss of control of the interview.

Think if you were a candidate and were asked, *"How do you deal with budgets?"* That is a pretty hard question to answer. Contrast that with, *"How did you put your first budget together when you were working at ABC?"*

The second question is easy to answer. There is no hesitation and it causes no added stress. The answer is specific behavioral data that helps predict future behavior. Tailor each of the interview questions for the specific person and situation.

4. Probing Questions

The fourth type of effective interview question is probing questions. Probing questions are defined as follow-up, clarification, and detail questions designed to gain more information. Jumping to conclusions and making assumptions are two of the biggest problems in an interview. This happens because some information is lacking. Asking additional and more specific questions results in a fuller picture.

A way to visualize the probing process is to think of the first question as the tip of the iceberg. To get all of the good information it is necessary to go below the surface. Keep digging for more data by asking probing questions. Here are some examples. *Who else worked on that project with you? How long did you work on the project? What was the budget for the project? Who had to approve the steps of the project? What changes were made to the project plan?*

Follow up, clarification and detail questions like those above lead to more and fuller data. The more data gained during the interview, the better and easier it is to make the hiring decision.

5. Example Questions

The fifth type of effective interview question is examples. Ask for examples of specific situations that are the same or similar to those the person will face on your job. Get an example of how the person reconciled accounts receivables if they will need to reconcile accounts receivables on your job.

Get an example of how they overcame a sales objection in a sales campaign if overcoming objections is important on your job. The best way to chronicle past behavior is by getting behavioral examples.

6. More Example Questions

The sixth category of effective interview questions, and the one most people have a hard time with, is more examples. Don't stop at one example. The Behavioral Model is accurate in predicting future behavior. However, the more examples of past behavior, the more accurate the prediction. The more times a person handles a situation or task a certain way, the greater the probability they will do it that way again in the future. Multiple behavioral examples are the best way to cement the behavioral pattern.

Get two or three examples of an objection they overcame in a sales campaign. Get two or three examples of a financial document they had to reconcile. Get two or three examples of a problem customer they handled.

To review, there are only six types of questions that should be asked in an interview. They are factual questions, action questions, candidate specific, probing, examples, and more examples.

Chapter Ten

Interview Questions

Part Three: Creating Questions

In this chapter the process of creating questions is explained. Creating great interview questions is not difficult if a proven process is used. Lack of preparation is the reason most people struggle with interview questions. Trying to create interview questions on the fly is always a mistake.

It is too difficult to create questions "real-time" during the interview. More time is spent thinking about the next question making it impossible to pay attention to the answer. Important information is missed as a result. And, it is very unlikely all of the requirements get fully explored.

The interview questions need to be prepared in advance of the interview. Here is a simple five-step process to create questions.

1. Begin With a Requirement

Go back to the Achievement-based Profile and review the list of requirements. That is the information necessary to predict success on the job. That work has already been done. Use a specific requirement as the starting point to develop an interview question.

2. Identify the Specific Piece of Data Needed

One of the characteristics of an effective question is it has specific, planned purpose. The AP identified the specific data needed to predict success. The definition of the requirement should be a clear statement of exactly what information is needed.

For an accounting position, the magic sentence question is, "How does someone with accounting skills behave?" The answer might be, "Someone who can reconcile monthly financial statements for 10K reports". That is the exact piece of data the question needs to unearth.

3. Look for an Opportunity the Person Had To Demonstrate the Requirement

Look at the information that is currently available for the candidate. This should include at a minimum a resume and/or an application. It might also include information from the phone screen or any additional submission gained through the screening process.

Sift through the information and look for opportunities the person had to demonstrate each specific requirement. Referring back to the accountant position, find situations where the person worked for a public company and was required to complete 10K reports. Find a project an engineering candidate worked on to explore project management skills.

4. Generate the Question

Create a specific question where the answer has to be the needed information. *"How did you prepare the last 10K report at ABC?" "How did you put the project plan together for the XYZ project?" "How did you get the appointment with the owner of the company at ABC?"* These are examples of questions that get specific, behavioral data.

5. Probe

Don't ever stop with the first question. Always dig for more information. Remember, the first question is the tip of the iceberg. Always ask more questions until the situation and the person's behavior is perfectly clear.

After asking, *"How did you prepare the last 10K?"* follow up with, *"How long did you work on the report?"* Then ask, *"Who helped you with the report?"* and *"How did you report the results?"*

Creating questions off the top of your head is hard and ineffective. Creating effective interview questions does not need to be a mystery or a chore. Follow this five-step process and creating effective interview questions is easy.

Interview Questions

Part Four: EARs

This chapter introduces one of the most powerful questioning techniques. It is called the EAR Technique. Remember the goal is to chronicle the person's past behavior to predict future behavior. The EAR technique is a way to organize interview questions into a logical pattern and gather behavioral examples.

E stands for Example

Find an example of a situation where the person had the opportunity to demonstrate the sought after behavior. For a salesperson, find an example of how they handle objections in a specific sales campaign. For an engineer, find an example of a project the person managed.

After the example is identified, it is necessary to probe. Ask as many questions as necessary until all of the circumstances of the situation are clear. Here are a number of examples of the types of probes that might be asked for the sales situation: *"How did you find the opportunity?"* *"What history did you have with the account?" "At what point in the sales campaign did the objection come up?" "Who brought up the objection?"*

It is important to know as much as possible about the example before moving to the next step. This helps to avoid assumptions.

A stands for Action

The next step is to determine how the person behaved in the situation. Ask questions that chronicle exactly how the person handled the situation. A good way to get into the action step of the EAR is to start your questions with the phrase 'step me through'. *"Step me through how you handled the price objection at ABC."* This forces a behavioral answer.

Once the person starts the answer, make certain to probe. Keep digging for more information to remove any ambiguity. It is critical to get the information needed and not necessarily what the person wants to share.

Here is a possible sequence using the handling objections example from above. If the response to your question is, *"The first thing I did was acknowledge the objection"* follow up with, *"What specifically did you say to them?"* Additional you might ask, *"How did you translate the objection into a value proposition?"* The more questions asked, the more data is gathered resulting in better hiring decisions.

R Stands for Result

A complete behavioral example includes the result of the person's behavior. What was the result of the situation? How did it turn out? A simple way to phrase the "R" question in our example might be, *"How did you know you had put the objection to rest?"*

Use the EAR model to find situations where the person had an opportunity to demonstrate the sought after behavior. Determine exactly how the person behaved in the situation. And, determine the outcome of the situation.

Armed with this data, the behavioral model predicts how the person will handle that same situation on your job. This makes the evaluation process simple. Evaluation is as simple as, "Will that behavior be successful on your job?"

The EAR technique is one of the most powerful ways to organize questions and get the information needed. The data gathering in an interview can be simplified to "**get as many EARS as possible**".

Chapter Ten

Interview Questions

Part Five: Interview Guide

An interview plan is essential to do a good interview. The term we use for the interview plan is **Interview Guide**. The Interview Guide is the list of questions in the order they will be asked.

As mentioned earlier, trying to figure out questions on the fly is almost impossible. Important information is missed and it makes listening very difficult. As a result, the lead-in questions for the interview need be prepared in advance. Most of the follow-up, clarification, and detail or probing questions will come as a result of the conversation.

Here is how the Interview Guide is prepared.

The first principle is to prepare the questions in correct chronological order. This means starting at the beginning of the person's career and working toward the present.

Too often people interview in reverse chronological. They start with the person's most recent job and continue backwards. Or even worse, there is no order at all to the questions. This results in bouncing all over the place. Neither of these are good models. Here is why interviewing in correct chronological order is critical.

First, an interview conducted in correct chronological order is the simplest way for the candidate to share information. They are sharing information the way it was imprinted on their brain. This makes it easy for them to recall and as a result there is far less stress.

Number two, interviewing in correct chronological order keeps the interview on track and helps to avoid getting lost. The process proceeds along a very logical timeline, the person's career.

The third reason to conduct interviews in correct chronological order is to identify trends and patterns. Spotting trends when working backwards is difficult. Look for trends to see if the person has reached a plateau in their career. It is never good to hire the person with ten years of experience that translates into one year of experience ten times.

Patterns of change, growth and learning are much easier to spot when interviewing in correct chronological order. Getting multiple EARs in consecutive time periods provides the best picture of how the person has grown in their career. It is very difficult to see those patterns when interview in reverse chronological order.

Begin putting the Interview Guide together by choosing the first time period. Freeze time and focus only on this time period. All of the questions are restricted to this one time frame. Generate a series of questions, and EARs related to the requirements around the candidate's experiences during that time frame. View the set of questions generated as a small, mini interview. Try to cover as many of the critical requirements as possible.

Once all the requirements are covered for the first time frame, move forward to the next time period and repeat the process. Generate a series of questions and EARs for the requirements around experiences during this time period. This is another small, mini interview.

Keep repeating the process until the entire background has been covered. An interview is a series of mini interviews. The most current experience is usually the most relevant. To incorporate this fact into the process, increase the number of questions as you move to the present. There may be six or eight questions for the first time period. There might be ten or twelve questions for the second time period. And, there might be 15 or 20 questions about their most recent job.

The result is a list of questions in the order they are to be asked. It is recommended the questions be printed double-spaced so there is a place to record the answers.

The Interview Guide is the map for the interview and ensures all the important information is gathered.

One question that is often asked is how far to go back in the person's career. Unfortunately, there is no standard answer to this question. There is an undeniable truth however that the more data collected, the better the hiring decisions. As a result, my advice is to go back as far as possible in the person's background. The farther back you go, the more trends and patterns can be identified.

There is an argument if the person has changed industries or professions the previous information is not important. This is simply not true. An EAR that explores the circumstances surrounding the change in careers can be critical. It is an example of decision-making skills. There is great behavioral data at all points in a person's background.

Use common sense, but try to go back a little bit farther than you think necessary.

In conclusion, the Interview Guide is a list of the interview questions in the order they will be asked. It acts as the roadmap for a great interview. It keeps the interview on track and helps to avoid missing information. And, it makes it easier to listen during the interview.

Chapter Ten

Interview Questions

Part Six: Questions to Avoid

No discussion of interview questions would be complete without pointing out the types of questions to avoid. And there are a lot of questions to avoid in interviews.

Unfortunately, there is a lot of misinformation in the market about interview questions. There are many myths that surround the subjects of interviewing and interview questions. And, certain of these myths have taken on a life of their own. Here are the types of questions to avoid.

The first type of question to avoid is open-ended questions. There was a discussion of why open-ended questions don't work in the section on the characteristics of effective questions. There are a couple of specific phrases that need to be avoided when creating questions. Don't start questions with, "Tell me about..." The result is almost always an open-ended question. The other phrase to avoid is, "Give me an example ..." Instead, ask for specific examples.

The way to fix open-ended questions is to make sure the question has only one answer. Instead of, *"Tell me about putting a project plan together,"* ask, *"How did you put together the construction project plan at ABC?"* Transform open-ended question by making certain there is only one answer.

The second type of interview question to avoid is theoretical questions. Theoretical questions make use of, "What if..." "What would you do if..." and then fill in the blank.

Theoretical questions share many of the faults of open-ended questions. In addition, the answer to a theoretical question is a theoretical answer. This requires some evaluation of theory which is a subject better left alone.

Also, theoretical questions promote canned responses. The answer to theoretical questions rarely help predict success.

Here is a technique to avoid theoretical questions. Make certain every question asked in the interview is in the past tense. Never ask the, "What would you do..." question. Instead, ask the, "What did you do?" question. Keep the questions in the past tense to get specific behavioral data.

The next category of questions to avoid is leading questions. Leading questions lead the person right to the answer. They telegraph the correct answer. Too often the answer to a leading question is not behavioral. Certainly the response isn't going to help predict success.

There are two techniques to stay away from leading questions. First, make sure the question is closed-ended and specific. Second, stay away from a long-winded preamble to the question. A good question does not need a build up.

"Here at Selecting Winners, we work very closely as part of teams. We are in pods that help each other solve problems and work on customer problems together. What type of environment do you work in?" What answer would you expect from this leading question? The candidate is going to repeat what they think you want to hear.

A great question is, *"Describe your work environment."* This is an effective, closed-ended question.

The next category of questions to avoid is "yes or no" questions. Yes or no questions as standalone questions don't provide a lot of information. In addition, they tend to cause the interviewer to jump to conclusions. A positive response to, *"Have you ever created a budget?"* causes people to assume the person has budgeting skills.

A better approach is to clearly identify the piece of data needed and design the question to get that piece of information. In this case ask, *"How did you prepare your last budget?"*

Yes or no questions cause more problems than they solve. Do everything possible to avoid them and instead go for specific behavioral questions.

The last category of questions to avoid is general, generic questions. These are difficult to answer. They don't result in specific information. They certainly won't help predict success.

Here is an example of a prelude to a general question. "Give me an example..." Why not just make it specific?

Instead of, *"Give me an example of a budget you have done,"* why not ask, *"Step me through how you completed the most recent budget at ABC"?*

This question makes it easy for the candidate to answer. It results in specific behavioral data and it is job related. Specific, behavioral questions are much better than general, generic questions.

To review, these are the types of questions to avoid:

- Open-ended questions
- Theoretical questions
- Leading questions
- Yes or no questions
- General questions.

Chapter Eleven

The Face-to-Face Interview

Part One: Interview Setting

In this section of the book we are going to cover the face-to-face interview. Interestingly enough, this is one of the shorter sections of the book. Everything completed to this point has been preparation. The Achievement-based Profile was created to know exactly what is needed on the job. It contains tremendous detail of both the expected outcomes and critical hiring requirements including the knowledge, skills, and behaviors necessary for the job.

In addition, the Interview Guide has a list of questions in the order they will be asked. The best strategy for the face-to-face interview is to work through the Interview Guide. Interviewing is actually very easy when all the preparation has been completed.

The interview setting is critical to an effective interview. There is great confusion about the right setting for an interview. There doesn't need to be.

The goal of the setting is to provide an environment conducive to exchange of information. That's it. An interview is a productive dialogue. Create an environment where a productive dialogue is easy to accomplish. Here are a couple of considerations.

The first consideration is privacy. The interview needs to take place behind closed doors. An open-air environment is never a good idea. Do whatever necessary to get behind closed doors. Borrow an office or reserve a conference room if you don't have an office. There is enough anxiety and tension in an interview without worrying about who is eavesdropping.

Second, avoid any kind of interruptions. Let people know about the interview. Someone walking into the office during the middle of an interview is unacceptable. This is one of the most important decisions made in your management career and running your business. Do not allow interruptions during the process.

Next, turn off the phone. Turn off everything that could be a distraction. One of the rudest things to do in an interview is take a phone call. 100% concentration is needed to effectively manage an interview.

Next, plan for time. Interviews need to be kept on track and on time. It is important to keep track of time during the interview without looking at a wristwatch. It is best to have a clock on the wall and have the candidate sit with their back to the clock. This makes it easy to track time without interrupting the flow of the interview.

Finally, avoid public places. Stay out of restaurants, bars and other public places. Eliminate as many distractions as possible. The interview is stressful enough for the candidate. And, it is important to have absolute concentration. It is hard to have a productive dialogue in a public place

This isn't meant to say a candidate can't be taken out to lunch or dinner. Feel free to wine and dine the candidate. However, the meal or drinks is more of a social event than a question and answer time.

There is a myth on the subject of the interview setting that needs to be put to rest. Much has been written over the years about the psychological barrier of a table between the interviewer and the candidate. The generally accepted advice has been there should not be any type of barrier. This is just plain hogwash. There is absolutely no truth to it.

The candidate needs to be as comfortable as possible. Use the environment appropriately. In all the years that I have interviewed, I have had a chair on the side of my desk so the candidate was on the side of my desk. That is just because that is the way it worked out with the configuration of my office.

Focus on putting the candidate at ease and having as productive a dialogue as possibly.

Chapter Eleven

The Face-to-Face Interview

Part Two: Opening

With the right environment, the next step is to open the interview properly. It is important to understand an interview is one of the most stressful situations a person ever encounters. The whole purpose of the opening is to reduce anxiety and establish rapport with the candidate.

The first step is to put the candidate at ease. It makes it easer to get better data when the candidate is comfortable. Don't believe anything about putting candidates under pressure or creating stress. Trying to get a read on a candidate by putting them under stress places you in a position for which you are not qualified. None of us are trained to interpret reactions under stress. This is a mistake. Put the candidate at ease to get the best data.

There are five things to do to effectively open the interview.

1. Break the ice

It is always nice to talk about the weather or parking or the directions or how they got there. Just use some small talk to establish a connection and break the ice with the individual. This eliminates some of the stress.

2. Explain the process

A huge component of the anxiety associated with an interview is fear of the unknown. The person is not sure what game is going to be played or from what direction the interviewer is coming. It is very helpful to explain the interview process. It puts the candidate at ease.

3. Mention notes

It is impossible to retain everything that transpires in an interview. Take notes to help recall all of the information. Note taking can cause anxiety if the candidate sees the interviewer start writing out of the blue. This won't happen if note taking is explained in the opening of the interview. There is no surprise and no anxiety as a result. Mention taking notes in the opening.

4. Clearly state the outcome

Tell the candidate exactly what is trying to be accomplished in the interview. Tell them how it will be conducted and what you hope to learn. These are all techniques to help put the candidate at ease.

5. Ask for questions

See if the candidate has any questions. At this point only accept questions about the process of the interview. Question about the company or the job should be held until the end of the interview.

Here is the exact script that I have used for 20 plus years to open every interview:

"Thank you for coming in today. We are going to spend some time covering your background. We are going to start at college and work our way to the present. I have a number of questions prepared to make certain we cover all the important areas. I will be taking notes so I don't forget any important information you share.

What I want to learn is how you handled the tasks and situations on your jobs so I can map that to how we do things here. The best thing you can do is fill in the details around my questions. Once we have worked to the present, we will spend some time discussing the position and company. Then I will answer any questions you might have. How does that sound?"

This script can be used to open every interview. Notice how the script breaks the ice and explains the process. It mentions taking notes and clearly states the outcomes. Finally, it asks for questions.

Chapter Eleven

The Face-to-Face Interview

Part Three: Controlling The Interview

Controlling an interview is as simple as getting the information needed in the allotted time. There is nothing more to it than that.

To control the interview it is necessary to control the agenda of the discussion. To control the agenda, ask effective questions, the types that we discussed in the section on questioning. When the candidate only has one possible answer, the conversation is being controlled.

Asking open-ended questions like, *"Tell me about business planning"* is the fastest way to lose control of the agenda.

Use the Interview Guide, the list of prepared questions, to manage and control the interview.

There is a lot of misinformation about controlling an interview. Don't get sidetracked by any of the crazy ideas about being in a position of power. The goal is to get as much quality data to help predict future behavior. Asking effective questions is all that is necessary to accomplish that goal.

Chapter Eleven

The Face-to-Face Interview

Part Four: Interviewing Tips

Here are some tips, techniques, and guidelines to help make the face-to-face interview more effective. The first tip is to forget all the games, gimmicks and tricks. There are so many people writing books and articles promoting different tricks and games that can be played in the interview. Unfortunately, any talk about games or gimmicks related to hiring employees is always a mistake.

Interviewing and choosing employees is a situation where there must be two winners. It is a win-win process. There cannot be a winner and a loser. If one party should fake out or deceive the other party and get the job by mistake, both parties end up losing. It doesn't work.

The relationship will fall apart very quickly if the hire is not a win for both the employer and employee. There cannot be any games, gimmicks or tricks. Dismiss any advice promoting games, gimmicks or tricks in an interview.

The next tip is to be wary of volunteered information. Candidates try to find a way to share information they want you to know. They are intent on sharing specific details. However, the Achievement-based Profile identifies the information that is needed. Stick to getting the necessary information to predict success and avoid everything else.

Stay in control of the interview. The information the candidate volunteers may be valuable, but more often than not it isn't. But if it does come up, fine, just move on. Go to the next question to regain control of the interview.

Next, if a tangent is productive pursue it. Interviews are difficult to control no matter how well planned. The conversation often takes an unpredictable course.

You might ask a sales candidate, *"What was the biggest deal you closed in the last quarter?"* The response might be, *"We were opening up a new vertical in healthcare."* Although discussing opening a new vertical market wasn't planned, this could be valuable information.

Always analyze if the tangent (the unplanned discussion) is a source of quality information. If the answer is yes, pursue it. The tangent represents an opportunity to get additional, quality data that helps predict success on the job.

When confronted with a positive tangent look to get an EAR covering how they chose the healthcare vertical, what plans they put together and who they have partnered with. If the tangent is not productive, cut off the answer and bring the conversation back to the original question.

The next interviewing tip is to take consistent notes. Note taking is a critical part of any good interview. It is difficult to retain everything that transpired in an interview. The goal is to record enough information so the conversation can be recreated. The information from the interview is used to complete the evaluation. A written record makes the evaluation easier to complete and more effective.

A helpful note taking technique is to fill in any gaps the minute the interview is over. Record as much information as possible while it is fresh. Go back through all the questions and fill in the answers.

There is a myth about breaking eye contact while taking notes. Most people think breaking eye contact with a candidate during the interview is rude. That is not correct. The candidate was told during the opening about notes so it is not a surprise. Also, the candidate gets to take a breath when eye contact is broken. The pressure is off when eye contact is broken so it turns into a positive. Take consistent notes.

Some people consider recording the interview instead of taking notes. First, there are legal considerations to recording conversations. The laws differ from jurisdiction to jurisdiction. Check with local counsel to learn the laws at your location. Second, the stress level almost always goes up when a recording device is introduced in an interview. The benefit of recording the interview seldom outweighs the increase in tension brought on by recording. Taking comprehensive notes is a better solution.

The last interviewing tip is the Interview Guide is gold. The list of questions, in the order they will be asked, is critical to a successful interview. It is almost impossible to conduct a quality interview without a list of questions prepared in advance. Take the time to prepare a comprehensive list of questions in advance.

Chapter Eleven

The Face-to-Face Interview

Part Five: Problem Situations

There are four problem situations that often come up in interviews. Eliminating these problems leads to a better interview and more information.

The first interview problem is long-winded answers by the candidate. It is like the dam burst after the question is asked. The candidate goes on and on with the answer. Unfortunately, control of the interview has been lost. There is a 2-part fix for this problem.

The first step is to determine if contained in the answer was the information needed. If so, interrupt and say, *"Thank you. That is what I was looking for."* Then ask the next question and control is regained. This interrupts the answer, but it is done very politely and regains control of the interview.

When the long-winded answer doesn't contain the needed information, interrupt and repeat the question to get the conversation back on track. "That is interesting, but what I'd like to know is..." and then repeat the question. A candidate rambling in the interview is counter-productive. Get the candidate and the interview back on track.

The second problem is the opposite problem. Sometimes the answer contains too little information. Many people get quiet when they are nervous. A good start to avoid this problem is to make sure the person is comfortable. Another technique to help the person open up is to be silent. Ask the question and be sure to give the candidate plenty of time to prepare the answer.

Don't jump in and repeat the question. Just ask the question and then allow the person time to respond. Also, encourage the person to elaborate.

This can be as simple as leaning forward as a gesture that encourages elaboration.

Finally, when getting very short choppy answers, ask specific questions that cannot be answered with a single word. *"How did you implement that new policy?"* That question cannot be answered in one or two words. Asking very focused, specific action questions requires the candidate to deliver longer answers.

The third interviewing problem is the candidate avoiding the question. This happens occasionally. Interrupt and repeat the same question if the candidate avoids the question. That sends a very powerful message.

It is generally good to give the candidate two opportunities to answer the question. If that doesn't work, the next step is to confront the behavior. Interrupt and say, *"I'm really trying to get an answer to this specific question. Is there a reason why we can't get an answer to this particular question?"*

I am not an advocate of confrontation. However, confronting the behavior when a candidate avoids the questions is an acceptable technique. Each question created is important. A specific piece of data is necessary and it is unacceptable to have the person avoid the question.

Finally, the fourth interview problem appears when a candidate loses their self-esteem. If they feel picked on, put down or made fun of, the interview ceases to be productive. It is the job of the interviewer to keep the candidate on an even keel and get quality information.

There are two techniques to help the candidate maintain self-esteem. The first is to offer a compliment early. In the first three to five minutes of the interview, compliment the candidate about a specific result. This causes the person to feel positive and results in better information.

The statement can be as simple as, *"I can see you worked very hard on that,"* or, *"That was a very nice result you got."* The candidate feels better, relaxes and as a result, you get better data. It is not necessary to compliment continuously throughout the interview, but once or maybe twice early in the interview makes a difference.

The second technique that helps maintain self-esteem is to show empathy. There are times in an interview it is necessary to go after negative information. A deadline missed, a mistake they made or lost sale are examples of negative information. These are legitimate behavioral situations to be explored. However, they can deflate a candidate.

The solution is to show empathy. One way to show empathy is to find common ground. With a salesperson you might say, *"Hey, there is always that one really big sale that gets away when you've been in sales as long as we have. Step me through the last big one that got away from you."*

Or, *"As busy as we are, there is always a deadline that is pretty difficult to meet. What was the last deadline you missed?"* This is much better than just asking, *"What was the last deadline you missed?"* That puts the candidate on the defensive and inhibits the productive exchange of information.

Those are ways to handle some of the more common problem situations that arise in an interview.

Chapter Eleven

The Face-to-Face Interview

Part Six: Closing the Interview

It is time to close the interview. All the prepared questions have been asked and answered. You have worked all the way through the person's background to the present.

The close of the interview is the time to market the position and the company. Some people might see this as counterintuitive. Too often people market the position and the company at the beginning of the interview. This is not a good idea for two major reasons.

1. At the beginning of the interview there is not enough information to know whether or not to market the job. Spending 20 or 30 minutes marketing the position and the company on the frontend is wasted time if it turns out the candidate is not a match.

    Common sense dictates to do whatever is necessary to get the candidate to agree to the interview. If this is a superstar from a direct competitor, it may be necessary to market like crazy just to get the person to come and talk. But, once they walk into the office, the goal is to gather data to determine whether or not to spend the time marketing.

2. The second reason to market at the end of the interview is there is not enough information to know how to effectively market the position and company before the interview. How do you sell to someone you know nothing about? What aspect of the job should be highlighted? How is it possible to put the best foot forward when nothing is known about the person? But by the end of the interview, you have learned what they are good at, where they got

excited and where they had the best success. Armed with this information, there is enough data to package the opportunity in a way that appeals to the candidate.

The time to market the position and the company is at the end the interview.

The close of the interview is also the time to answer the candidate's questions. During the interview, only questions about the actual process were answered. The reason to wait until the close of the interview is because you don't know how much time to spend answering the candidate's questions.

Take as long as necessary answering questions for the tremendous candidate. Go into as much depth and detail as necessary for the best candidates. However, for the weak candidate, answering a lot of questions isn't a good use of time. This determination cannot be made at the beginning of the interview.

After answering the candidate's questions, explain the next step in the process. Tell the candidate exactly what is going to happen and when it will happen. *"We have three more people to interview. At that point we will decide who will be brought back. You will hear back from us by the end of the week if we are going to go to the next step."* That is one possible scenario.

Another scenario to use with a fabulous candidate is, *"Listen, I would really like you to speak to members of the team and the vice president of the department. We would like to schedule that as soon as possible. Can you take a look at your calendar to see when you might be able to get back in?"* The discussion is about the next steps.

And, keep any commitments made. If a commitment is made to get back to them by the end of the week, get back to them by the end of the week. Even if an answer is not available say, *"I'm sorry. It is going to take us a few more days to make a decision."* But if a promise is made to get back to them, then get back to them.

The last note on the close of the interview is to end it on a friendly note. Treat everyone who walks through the door with absolute, total respect. There may be candidates who don't meet the requirements but they are human beings and deserve to be treated as such.

Besides, it is in the best interest of your company to treat everyone with respect. It is never good to have people walking the streets saying negative things about your organization. This is part of building a positive reputation for the company. Treat everyone with absolute total respect and end it on a friendly note whether or not the person will be going to the next step.

The close of the interview is the time to market the position and company, answer the candidate's questions, explain the next step and end it on a friendly note.

Chapter Twelve

Marketing The Position

This chapter covers a few tips on marketing the position to a candidate. As mentioned previously, the time to market the position and company is at the end of the interview. That is when there is enough information about the candidate to package the job appropriately.

The pitch needs to be tailored to the specific person. A canned pitch usually doesn't work.

One of the best ways to tailor the pitch is to match opportunities to successes. A number of situations where the person was successful were identified during the interview. It might have been selling at high levels. It might have been creating financial forms. Whatever it might have been, these were environments and situations where the person was successful.

Success is addictive. Match the opportunities your position offers to successes the person had in the past. Make sure to put opportunities to sell at a high level as a prominent component of the pitch if the person has been successful selling at the highest levels.

But, make sure to paint the real picture. Share the positives of the position as well as the negatives. It may sound strange to share negatives with a candidate when marketing a position, but it is an important idea.

Only sharing the positives leads to disappointment when person comes on board and experiences the negatives. It may be the company is very bureaucratic or there is lots of paperwork or there are lots of politics. This leads to frustration and a good chance the person leaves.

However, painting an honest picture including positives and negatives leads to better decisions. A great example of this occurred early in my career. I was recruiting high tech employees into a data center for an organization. This data center was absolute state of the art with the latest and the greatest equipment.

When marketing to candidates, it was stressed they would have an opportunity to work with the latest and greatest equipment. But I also mentioned that the company is a big company, very bureaucratic and there are lots of politics. It was important to show the positives and the negatives so there were no surprises. Armed with both the good and the bad, the person could make a better decision.

Another important marketing concept is to share the relationship between success and rewards. Let people know the expected outcomes listed on the Achievement-based Profile. Then tie the rewards to those accomplishments. Share the relationship between what they can accomplish and how they will be rewarded.

Another way to discuss rewards is called social proof. This is subtle but effective. Illustrate how other people have been rewarded for achieving similar results.

"Fred is our top salesperson. He did this. This is what he got. Sally was our #2 salesperson and this is what she did. This is what she got." That is social proof. If they see other people doing it, it is proof that the rewards are real.

It is important not under or over promise when marketing the position. Be as realistic as possible.

Finally, personalize it. This is a person. Recruiting is all about relationships. Personalize your marketing wherever possible.

These simple tips help when marketing your job.

Chapter Thirteen

References

Good hiring decisions are based on good quality data. Large quantities of information were gathered during the interview. The next step is to validate the interview data and make sure it is of the highest quality.

One critical step to validate the data is with reference checks. This has been a very controversial subject, but it doesn't need to be. Reference checks are critical to making good hiring decisions. Making a hiring decision without doing a reference check is a disservice to the organization.

The purpose of a reference check is to verify the interview data and gather additional data. Before we go any farther let's talk about legalities.

As of the writing of this book, checking references is legal in all 50 states in the United States. There are varying rules, but it is legal. I am not an attorney and I am not dispensing legal advice. My advice is to check with your local counsel to get the guidelines for your particular state. However, a company has the right to check references on candidates.

Here a list of dos and don'ts for reference checking to get the most value out of the process and also keep out of trouble.

The first thing to do is get a release from the reference. There are formal forms that can be found online. Or simply have the candidate provide the reference information. The candidate can provide a document or an email with reference contact information. This works in most cases as a release. But once again, check with your counsel.

Don't just get the contact information. Have the candidate do as much of the work as possible. Have the candidate contact the references and tell them who you are and why you will be calling. This makes the job of checking references much easier.

The types of people to get as references are those who can speak to the quality and quantity of work the person has done. Do not look for character references. Don't talk to their priest, their rabbi or their neighbor. Only speak with people who can speak to the quality and quantity of work the person has done.

This usually includes past supervisors, coworkers, and subordinates. In some cases you might speaking with customers or vendors.

The next step is to identify the areas of inquiry. Go back to the interview notes and identify the data that needs to be confirmed. If the person said they had responsibility for a $2 million budget, that might be a data point to validate. If they said they worked on a sale for three months, validate that piece of data.

Next, develop a list of effective questions. The types of questions to ask in the reference check are exactly the same types that are asked in the interview. Ask effective, behavioral, closed-ended questions.

If the person said they had a $3 million budget, the question to ask is, *"What was the size of the person's budget?"* That is a nice, effective, closed-ended and factual question.

During the reference check make certain to listen actively and probe. Ask follow-up, clarification, and detail questions to eliminate any ambiguity.

There are some areas that need to be avoided in the reference check. Don't ask general questions. *"Tell me about Barry."* That is a waste of time.

Don't make assumptions in the reference check. Follow up to get full information. Probing is essential in the reference check. If the person says, *"They had responsibility for the project."* Follow up by asking who else was involved in the project. Who did they report to? What was the size of the budget of the project? Keep digging with questions to get more information wherever possible.

There are a couple of areas of danger when conducting reference checks. The first is conducting secondary references. A secondary reference is when information is sought from a person you don't have permission to speak with.

Here is a typical path to secondary references. The candidate provides Person A as a reference. At the end of that reference you might say, *"Hey, do you know anybody else who knows this person?"* The response is, *"Sure, Person B."*

Person B his is a secondary reference. No permission was given to talk to Person B. This is a very dangerous situation. The problem lies with Person B's loyalties. Person B might have a connection to someone at the candidate's place of employment. They could call back to the candidate's place of employment and create a very difficult situation.

Some practitioners contend the only way to get good references is by talking to secondary references. That is absolutely not true. Secondary references are dangerous and should be avoided.

The last area of danger when conducting reference checks is asking for opinions or judgments. Everyone understands there is a built-in bias in reference checking. People don't give their enemies as references. The assumption is anyone the candidate gives as a reference has a predisposition to say nice things about the candidate. This is true but does not need to be a problem.

The way to eliminate the bias is to never ask for an opinion or a judgment. If you ask, *"Is Barry a good manager?"* The answer is going to be full of wonderful things. This is to be expected. The effective technique is to never give them that opportunity.

Instead of asking for opinion, ask, *"How many people did Barry manage? How many of those people did he hire? Who was the last problem person that Barry dealt with? How did he deal with that person?"*

These are all effective closed-ended questions. The person responding to these questions never has the opportunity to say anything nice. With closed-ended questions, there is only one answer.

Follow these do's and don'ts when conducting reference checks.

Chapter Fourteen

Background Checks

Background checks are an important step in the selection process. They protect both the manger and the organization. The best advice is to hire a professional firm. There are many firms both local and national. They are easily identified online or in the local yellow pages. They should provide all the release forms and procedures.

Most of the background work these days is database work. It is very quick. In most cases, 24-hour turnaround time can be expected. Also, background check services are very inexpensive. My recommendation is to do a background check on every single candidate considered for employment.

Background checks validate information to help protect the organization. Typical things to check are criminal backgrounds, driving records, degrees, credentials and financial information. Be certain that any information checked is job related because there are laws governing what can and cannot be checked.

Once again, my recommendation is to employ the services of either a local or a national firm. Walk through the process with them and then run the process by your counsel. Complete a background check on every candidate considered to be hired in the organization.

Chapter Fifteen

The Hiring Decision

The last step is to make the hiring decision. Believe it or not, making the hiring decisions is simple. What makes it simple is the volumes of data collected during the process.

There is a four-step process for making the hiring decision.

1. Gather All The Data

Think about all the sources of data. There is the resume and/or application. There are any additional submissions that might have been submitted. There is the data from the phone screen. There is the data from the face-to-face interview. There is the data from any additional interviewers. There is the reference check and background check data. There is testing or assessment data if any was completed. Gather all the data.

2. Gather The Team

Anybody who was involved in the selection process should contribute to the decision. They contribute data to help evaluate each requirement

3. Evaluate One Requirement At a Time

Instead of an overall evaluation, evaluate one critical requirement at a time. The goal is to break a massive evaluation job into a series of smaller, more manageable pieces. Each person on the interview team has input into the evaluation. They contribute for those requirements they covered in the interview.

4. Substantiate the Evaluation With Data

Subjectivity needs to be minimized when making hiring decision. Substantiating the evaluation with data from the interview accomplishes this. Don't just say, *"Barry has very good presentation skills."* Instead say, *"Barry has very good presentation skills as evidenced by the ABC presentation. Here is how he prepared. It was delivered to this specific audience. Here is how he responded to questions. Here is the result he achieved as a result of the presentation."*

Use the data gained from the EARs in the interview to support the evaluation. Using EARs eliminates the greatest majority of the subjectivity because the requirements have to be substantiated with behavioral examples.

As far as the actual grade itself, there are all kinds of complicated formulas. The simplest is an evaluation grid. Across the top, the individual requirements are listed. Down the left hand side the candidates are listed. Work horizontally across the grid.

KEY ✓ = Meets requirement + = Exceeds requirement — = Exceeds requirement	Requirements							Comments
Candidate								

For each candidate, evaluate one requirement at a time. The actual grades to use are:

Meets the requirement = ✔

Exceeds the requirement = +

Does not meet the requirement = –

If they meet the requirement the grade is a check ✔. If they exceed the requirement the grade is a plus (+). And if they do not meet the requirement the grade is a minus (-).

This is very simple, straightforward and it is visual. There is a tremendous amount of research supporting the fact people cannot be evaluated to a greater level of granularity than meets, exceeds, or does not meet.

If you want to use a '1 to 10' system, what is the difference between a '6' and a '7'? Are you a hard grader or an easy grader? It gets very complicated. The system of ✔, +, – is simple and effective.

A couple of notes: If there is a minus anywhere in the row, by definition, the person is going to fail. Remember, every one of the requirements is a must. There are no 'nice to haves' on the Achievement-based Profile. The definition of the must is if they do not have this, they don't get hired.

It is easy to determine whether or not the person will be successful on the job by simply looking at the grid.

There are questions about breaking ties. The truth is I don't know how to break ties because I have never seen one. I have never seen two equal candidates using this system. It becomes very obvious whether or not the person will succeed in the position viewing the evaluation grid.

Make it as simple as possible. Gather all the data. Gather the interview team. Evaluate one requirement at a time. Substantiate the evaluation with data and then map it out on the grid with the requirements across the top and the candidates down the left hand side. Work horizontally using the grades meets, exceeds or does not meet.

Making the hiring decision is very easy. Decisions are now made based on volumes of data. It has been my experience that using this model eliminates agonizing over hiring decisions.

Chapter Sixteen

Making the Offer

Now is the time to make the offer.

There are a couple of things to remember in putting together the job offer. The offer needs to be a win-win. A great way to think of the employment relationship is as a **behavior rental agreement**. The company is renting the candidate's behavior in return for specific business results. It is a trade of money, benefits, and a successful work environment for business results.

The relationship needs to be win-win. Depending on market conditions, there are opportunities to take advantage of candidates. Here is an example. If the job is worth $50,000 to the organization and the candidate is currently making $35,000 a year, most people think it would be nuts to offer somebody $50,000 when they are currently making $35,000.

However, if the job is worth $50,000, pay the person $50,000. If the person is hired at $40,000, they will find out that everybody else is making $50,000. They will learn they could make $50,000 elsewhere doing the same exact thing. How long are they going to stay?

Win-win means a fair wage is paid, not the least amount you can get away with. And in return excellent performance is expected. Do everything possible to create win-win situations.

In addition, anticipate that the person will get a counter offer from their existing employer. This is very likely with top performers. Deal with the subject of counter offers on the front end.

There are two strategies for dealing with counter offers. First, discuss it with the candidate. Ask the candidate if they think their current company will counter this offer when they give notice. Have a discussion about it in advance.

The second strategy is to follow up. From the moment the offer is made until the person walks in on their first day on the job, try to have constant contact. Stay in the forefront of their mind. Start to treat them as part of the team before they arrive. That counteracts some of the efforts the other organization makes to keep the person.

The final issue with a job offer is it must be in writing. Do not make job offers verbally. Your in-house counsel will tell you the same thing. This eliminates any "He said, She said." There will be no misunderstandings. Everything is in writing. The candidate should sign the offer and return it so everybody has agreed to the exact same set of terms.

The most important thing with an offer is to make sure it is a win-win for both the company and the new employee.

Chapter Seventeen

Onboard

The final step is to get the person onboard and on the road to success. The HR types have actually come up with a name for this. They call it onboarding. Here are a couple of tips that help get the relationship off to a great start.

1. Prepare for success. Have a plan in place to get the person up to speed. Have all the logistics including their workspace in place. Be prepared for the person to come on board and be successful.
2. Have clear expectations. Go back to the Achievement-based Profile and review the list of short, medium, and long term expected outcomes. Have this list of expected outcomes ready to discuss with the new employee. Set very clear expectations.

It has been my experience that most management problems are a direct result of mismatched expectations. Make the expectations as clear as possible. The good news is the outcomes and expectations are already written in the AP.

One final thought on bringing the person on board. Create a situation where the new person can have an early success. The first assignment for the person has to be an assignment you are absolutely certain they will complete successfully. Make sure it is short in duration and very concise.

There is nothing better than kicking off a relationship with a good, positive experience. Success breeds success.

At this point a new employee has been hired who has the highest probability of being successful. You have gone through a process that is straightforward, clear and easy to execute. The outcome is the right person in the right job at the right time doing the right things. The personal benefit is far less employee headaches and a much greater return on your entire investment.

Appendix A

Sample Interview Questions

Below are a number of sample interview questions. Review these and notice how they fall into one of the 6 effective question types. These can be used as a starting point when developing questions for the interview. DO NOT fall into the trap of using these without customizing. Each question should be tailored to the individual person and situation.

SALES

By what percentage did you increase sales last year?
How many sales did you complete last month?
What strategy did you use to close the ABC deal?
How did you overcome the price objection in the ABC sale?
What have you done in the past 6 months to improve your sales skills?

ADMINISTRATIVE

What was the most complicated document you created in the last month?
What changes did you make to the filing system?
What system did you use to manage your day yesterday?
What percentage of your day is spent on the phone?
What deadlines have you faced this week?

MANAGEMENT

How many people have you hired on this job?
Describe how you handled the last problem employee.
Step me through how you created this year's budget.
How did you establish credibility with your team when you took the job?
How did you implement the last change in policy with your team?

TECHNICAL

How did you troubleshoot the new software?
How did you fix the last equipment failure you faced?
What was your specific role on the design team?
How did you calculate the tolerance variations on the ABC project?
What was the last new technical skill you developed?

INTERPERSONAL BEHAVIORS

What was your key contribution to the team? (Teamwork)
How have you kept your projects on track? (Flexibility)
Describe the last time you went above and beyond to help a customer. (Initiative)
How did you get the team members to work together? (Leadership)
How did you get the machine up and running? (Problem-solving)
How did you make certain you understood the customer's concern? (Listening)

Appendix B

The Achievement-based Profile

Selecting Winners

Achievement-based Success Profile

POSITION	REPORTS TO	DEPARTMENT	OPENING DATE

RESEARCH CHECKLIST

- ❑ REVIEW CURRENT JOB DESCRIPTION
- ❑ REVIEW PREVIOUS POSITION PROFILE
- ❑ ANALYZE THE JOB
- ❑ OBSERVE THE JOB

- ❑ TALK TO INTERNAL EXPERTS
- ❑ TALK TO EXTERNAL EXPERTS
- ❑ PROFILE SUCCESSFUL PEOPLE
- ❑ PROFILE UNSUCCESSFUL PEOPLE

ACHIEVEMENT-BASED OUTCOMES

To predict if someone will be successful you must first define success. You do this by clearly outlining your achievement-based outcomes, which we call expectations. First, determine your short-term expectations. Short-term should be defined by you. Answer the question, "What must the person accomplish for you to label them a success?" Repeat these steps for the medium-term and the long-term. The results are the outcomes necessary for success and are a key component of our profile.

SHORT-TERM EXPECTATIONS

MEDIUM-TERM EXPECTATIONS

LONG-TERM EXPECTATIONS

Achievement-based Success Profile

ACHIEVEMENT-BASED BEHAVIORS (REQUIREMENTS)

The critical requirements for success are stated in terms of achievement-based behaviors. These will fall in two general categories. First are "quantitative" which are the requirements that we can easily measure (e.g. typing, foreign language, presentation skills, etc.) Second are "qualitative" which describe the behaviors necessary for success. Gut-feel, chemistry, fit and attitude need to be translated to the behaviors. Flexibility, leadership and creativity are examples of qualitative requirements. Use the magic sentence, "How does someone with _____ behave?", to define each label.

REQUIREMENT / LABEL	MUST	DEFINITION & RECOGNITION

Achievement-based Success Profile

REQUIREMENT / LABEL	MUST	DEFINITION & RECOGNITION

Selecting Winners

Achievement-based Success Profile

Key						COMMENTS
✓ = meets requirement						
+ = exceeds requirement						
— = does not meet requirement						

CANDIDATES	ACHIEVEMENT-BASED BEHAVIORS	COMMENTS